MW00478125

GANGLAND

Crimes of the Century

Hitler's Englishman: The Crime of Lord Haw-Haw
Rotten to the Core? The Life and Death of Neville Heath

GANGLAND

THE CASE OF
BENTLEY AND CRAIG

Francis Selwyn

ROUTLEDGE

First published in 1988 by
Routledge
11 New Fetter Lane, London EC4P 4EE

Printed in Great Britain by Billings & Sons Ltd, Worcester

British Library Cataloguing in Publication Data
Selwyn, Francis
    Gangland: the case of Bentley and Craig.—
    (Crimes of the century).
    1.   Great Britain. Murder. Trial of Bentley,
    Derek. Craig, Christopher
    I.   Title   II.   Series
    344.205′2523′0922

ISBN 0–415–00907–3

This account of the Craig and Bentley case acknowledges the part played in it by Anne Doran, John McEwan, and John Rees among many others whose names are not recorded.

CONTENTS

PREFACE

To write of the Craig and Bentley case in the autumn of 1987 is to relive the events of the autumn of 1952 but also, fortuitously, to experience something of the same atmosphere of public indignation at a threat to the basic decencies of English life. In 1952 it was a matter of hysteria over the rising tide of armed robbery and gangland violence, the streets of England's cities turned into a moral replica of Capone's Chicago. The press and the spokesmen for the nation's natural leaders assured the country that it was so. Later on this proved to be false, but the moralists were unrepentant. 'Statistics should be disregarded,' suggested one of them in *The Times* on 22 January 1953, 'in favour of general experience and general opinion.' Six days later a mentally subnormal youth, nineteen years old, was hanged for a murder he did not commit and which was known by all concerned to have been committed about quarter of an hour after he was arrested. The House of Commons was told beforehand that it was forbidden to discuss whether or not he ought to be executed until he had been executed.

In 1987 no one is in danger of being hanged for child abuse. Yet the manner in which its incidence is discussed has disquieting similarities to that other public anxiety in the autumn of 1952. The crime exists, but its extent is obscured by shrill and prurient headlines, 'estimates' of figures that always show an implacable rate of increase, a reticence in defining the precise frontiers of the offence (as if no nice person could possibly want to know), the inclusion of reports, false alarms, and children thought to be 'at risk,' as if they were proven instances. As in 1952, scepticism is unwelcome. On 6 October, *The Times* reports a senior official of the social services as denouncing parents, police, lawyers, doctors, and those who challenged the findings of the social services in the case of individual children. By their objections that justice was not being done and no offence had been committed, by going to court to prove it, they were themselves responsible for a further 'abuse of the children'.

Such a period of public concern is no time for dissent or a demand to know precisely what the offence consists of and whether the figures bear impartial examination. Those who suggested such things in 1952, as in 1987, were seen as being indifferent to the immediate plight of the victims and instinctively on the side of the wicked. As Dryden made Titus Oates say, three centuries ago, of those who queried whether the guilty men executed for the Popish Plot might not be innocent after all:

> The wretch who did me such a dire disgrace,
> Should whet my memory, though once forgot,
> To make him an Appendix of my Plot.

But 1952 and 1987 were unlike in a single important aspect. However great the injustice in the case of Craig and Bentley, or Ruth Ellis, or Timothy Evans, there was a sense that this was the last spasm of an authoritarian philosophy. Enlightenment and liberalism lay ahead. A new and more humane outlook in public affairs would, among other libertarian gestures, abolish hanging and curtail censorship. The second consideration was directly relevant at a time when books, comics and films were glibly presented as the inspiration of crime. By contrast, the events of 1987, whatever their outcome, have as their background a society moving from libertarianism to a period of authoritarian instincts. From government and media, from populist right or feminist left, the authoritarian voices increasingly prevail, however differing their creeds. Investigative reporting creates a back-up law enforcement within television and journalism, while watchdogs bark at the first sign of artistic impropriety on the screen. There prevails in that respect what was once called the 'pedal cyclist' mentality of bowing the back to those above and treading on those below. Never was Lord Reith's moral philosophy more evident than that of the arbiters who decide that the danger of Aids or the imperative of sexual equality must be inserted into situation comedy or soap opera. In a broader political sense, the individual is more accountable to the state for the conduct of his or her private life.

The account of the Craig and Bentley case which follows is set against the social background of its day, the movements in popular culture and moral attitudes, the fervour for law and order combined with a certain indifference to the occurrence of crime. To see the case in this light makes it more cautionary rather than less. Its relevance and challenge to our own beliefs about society and its enemies remain undiminished.

CHAPTER 1

The story of the most disturbing and controversial murder case during the post-war years followed in the wake of two other crimes. In one respect it was the consequence of these two armed robberies. Indeed, it had a direct family connection with them.

The first case culminated in a banner headline across the front page of the *Daily Herald* on 31 October 1952: DEAD HAND JAILED COLDEST GUNMAN. With an assurance that a thriller writer might envy, the paper added, 'The fingerprint of a dead gunman who refused to squeal while alive, yesterday jailed for 12 years one of Britain's most cold-blooded criminals.' Inset was a picture of a young man, a soft and immature face with an uncertain expression. It claimed the second headline: YOUNG, DANGEROUS BABY-FACE.

Neither Derek Bentley nor, perhaps, Christopher Craig was directly involved in the crime. Yet it was Baby-Face's widely-reported armed robbery that began a sequence of events leading one of them to the gallows at Wandsworth.

For its victims, the visit of Baby-Face and his friends to their home on a winter's night was a classic nightmare of modern crime, a situation of personal terror exploited by cinema melodrama from that day to this.

Mr and Mrs Herbert Whiten were a couple with a small child who lived at 55 Honey Lane, Waltham Abbey, on the outer fringe of north-east London. During the night of 14–15 March 1952, an American car – a large Buick – pulled up outside the house and the driver turned off the engine. He and his four passengers got out. It was then a little after midnight. A few minutes later, the Whitens woke to find torches shining in their faces and the bed surrounded by five men wearing trilby hats and scarves wound round their faces as masks. The driver of the car aimed a Luger automatic pistol at the startled and frightened couple, demanding the keys to the safe.

In the next half hour, the clichés of film terror came true for Herbert Whiten and his wife. The keys to the safe were not in their home. So the raiders tied up the couple, cut the telephone wires and ransacked the house. But, with the moral irony of a Hollywood gangster movie, the masked robbers came away with only £4 in cash, a cigarette lighter taken from Mr Whiten's trouser pocket, and some Scroll ballpoint pens. For all the gun-waving and the sardonic threats, this particular crime had been grotesquely ill-organised and even worse carried out. But the frightened couple were only too thankful to have the ordeal over and to have escaped without any worse injury.

At 3am, the Buick was found abandoned and inexplicably overturned three miles from Waltham Abbey. Of the robbers, there was no sign. One of them had left a bicycle-lamp in the car and this was taken for fingerprinting. However, not far away a police patrol spotted a man on foot. He was recognised at once as a local villain, George Albert King, *alias* Ginger King, *alias* Cat's Eyes King. The nickname of Cat's Eyes had nothing to do with keenness of vision. Indeed, he suffered from night-blindness. But he had learnt to drive at speed through the darkness by keeping the outer wheels of the car on the cat's-eyes reflectors that studded the central division of the carriageway. By steering in this manner, he was able to follow the curves and turns of the road without actually seeing where he was going. Hence, presumably, the overturned Buick.

Ginger King's arrest was a bonus for Scotland Yard in one respect, since he was already wanted for his part in an £8,000 mailbag robbery. He was a professional thief, but the level of his professionalism was open to question. In his pocket there was a Scroll ballpoint pen matching those stolen at Waltham Abbey, found when he was searched at the police station. The bicycle-lamp in the abandoned Buick had his fingerprints on it. He was arrested, charged, and faced trial on his own without revealing the names of the other armed robbers. He went down for a lengthy term of imprisonment, which he knew he would never serve. Not only was King night-blind, he was also in the final stages of tuberculosis. He died in prison six months later.

The ownership of the car was known to the police from the vehicle's registration. It was registered in the name of Cyril Burney, twenty-seven years old, known equally well to the military police and their civilian colleagues. But he was not the car's owner. It had been purchased a few weeks before for £200 by Niven Scott Craig, twenty-six years old and already the subject of an impressive file in the Criminal Records Office. He seemed to be that most dangerous of law-breakers, the bright middle-class boy turned to crime. As a child of ten or so in South London, he had won a scholarship to Archbishop Tenison's Grammar School. By the age of fourteen he was convicted of store-breaking and sent to an approved school. He escaped and went on the run with a stolen firearm.

After leaving school he volunteered for military service while still technically under age. In 1947, serving with the Gordon Highlanders, he was court-martialled in Austria on charges of armed robbery. Sentenced to five years' imprisonment, he escaped from his escort and made his way to Italy, where he staged four armed hold-ups on drivers of military vehicles, making off with the vehicles and their contents. By the time that he was discharged from the army, he had twelve convictions for military offences. Since then, he had become well known to the police and the civil courts. Despite the photograph on the front page of the *Daily Herald*, by 1952 he had shed something of the Baby-Face look. He was pictured elsewhere as a dark, smartly-dressed young man with a David Niven moustache. He was known in the underworld as 'The Velvet Kid' and had the reputation of liking to be seen about the West End with 'glamorous-looking show girls'.

Like Ginger King, whatever his professional ambitions, his latest crime had been that of an amateur. In common with his younger brother and Derek Bentley, his career as a criminal was less rewarding than most legitimate ways of making money. The robbery in Honey Lane had been bungled and well-nigh pointless. Within a few hours, the wrecked Buick gave him away. By wrecking and abandoning the car, he and Burney had announced their presence to the police. By leaving the bicycle-lamp in the wreck and carrying the incriminating ballpoint pen in his pocket, Ginger King had done the rest.

Niven Craig and Burney went on the run together. The *Daily Mirror* reported the armed robbery at Waltham Abbey and published a picture of the wrecked Buick with the number-plate clearly legible. Craig and Burney knew the hunt for them was on. Cyril Burney proved to be more adept in making crime pay. He was also wanted for an £800 fur robbery at Wembley and was apparently living on the proceeds. Scotland Yard, following what information and sightings it could get, trailed Niven Craig and Cyril Burney during the spring and summer of 1952. It was six months to the day after the Waltham Abbey robbery that the hunters made their capture.

On 14 September, at half-past two in the afternoon, the Yard received information that Niven Craig and Cyril Burney were lying low in a Bayswater apartment. It was in one of the tall houses of Kensington Park Gardens just off the main shopping street of Queensway, behind Whiteley's department store. The fugitives still seem to have been living on the sale of stolen furs, some of which were found in the house. The Yard's information was that both men were armed and likely to use their guns unless taken by surprise.

Detective-Sergeant William Lewis and Sergeant Cook were to carry out the arrests, under the command of their inspector and with a police driver. They went up to a room on the second floor of the Bayswater house but found the door locked. Then there was the sound of a window being opened and the sight of Cyril Burney making his escape by way of the drainpipe. Lewis and Cook raced down the stairs and caught him as he was climbing a ladder into the rear mews. There was a violent struggle, which ended with Burney being taken up to his room again in handcuffs. It was here that a number of the stolen furs still lay.

The door of the other room remained locked, when Lewis tried it again. But in response to his knock, it was presently opened by a woman. Niven Craig was lying on the bed and had apparently just woken up. Followed by Cook, Lewis dashed in and later described the sequel.

'I brushed past her into the room and saw Craig lying on his back on a bed. He sat up and immediately put his right hand under the pillow. I jumped for the head of the bed and put my hand under the pillow and took from his hand an automatic pistol.'

Though Niven Craig had bleached his hair in an attempt at disguise, Lewis had not the least doubt of his identity. The encounter that followed was short and decisive, which was just as well since the pistol was both loaded and cocked. Several rounds of ammunition were also found in Niven Craig's pockets. Like Burney, he was handcuffed and taken away. Three of the five robbers at Waltham Abbey had been accounted for. That was as far as the police were able to get by September.

Niven Craig was charged with the Waltham Abbey robbery and possessing an automatic pistol with intent to endanger life. A third charge of stealing or receiving a driving licence was not proceeded with. At the Central Criminal Court in October he and Burney pleaded not guilty. Craig's defence was that he and his sixteen-year-old brother, Christopher Craig, had been staying with a friend at Wells-on-Sea in Norfolk at the time of the Waltham Abbey crime. The friend was called in support of this. But the details of his arrest told a story of their own and the jurors did not believe him. After his conviction and the revelation of his previous criminal history, their scepticism must have seemed justified. Even if his alibi was genuine, the evidence of the gun under his pillow destroyed any probability that he was an innocent man wrongly accused.

The girl who was with him in the Bayswater room told a different story. She did not tell it in court, wrote Christopher Craig's counsel John Parris, having convictions of her own for prostitution. She and Niven Craig had been in bed and asleep when the knock came on the door. She got up and opened it. Sergeant Lewis was across the room and his hand under the pillow before Craig could do anything. Lewis himself drew out the gun, saying to Craig, 'Now what would a nice boy like you want with a thing like this?'

Even if true, it would not have saved Craig from prison. Innocent men, in the opinion of jurors, do not sleep with guns under their pillows.

Scotland Yard was well satisfied with the outcome of the case. Christopher Craig, who left the court with his mother after his elder brother had been sent down for twelve years, was to remember overhearing one policeman saying to another on the steps of the Old Bailey, 'Well, we've got rid of that bugger for a bit.' In the light of the press coverage of the trial, it was a satisfaction likely to have been shared by the great majority of Fleet Street's readers. It was later suggested that the remark had been made deliberately in the hearing of the family as a taunt.

Mr Justice Hilbery had passed sentence on 30 October. Next day the press carried his remarks, made to Niven Craig who stood before him in the dock. Though the judge spoke to one criminal, there was a sense in which he also identified a more general and frightening trait in post-war crime, pronouncing judgment on a new generation of the violent young.

'I have watched you carefully in the course of this trial,' he said to Craig, 'and I can say with regard to both matters of which you stand convicted I do not remember, in the course of some seventeen years on the Bench trying crimes of violence, a young man of your age who struck me as being so determined as you have impressed me as being.'

Niven Craig's determination, in Mr Justice Hilbery's view, was of a terrifying kind.

'You are not only cold-blooded, but from my observation of you I have not the least hesitation in saying I believe that you would shoot down, if you had the opportunity to do so, any police officer who was attempting to arrest you or indeed any lawful citizen who tried to prevent you from committing some felony which you had in hand. I have little doubt that it was you who held the gun and that these others were men of rougher material, at any rate the man standing by your side in the dock acting under your directions.'

Though Niven Craig was the star of this particular drama, the judge's comments to Cyril Burney made the point that criminals of this stamp were no longer exceptional.

'You are quite obviously a bad character. On your record it is quite clear you are not prepared to submit to the ordinary necessary disciplines which the law-abiding citizen must necessarily submit to, if he is to live in such a society as ours. You too are a dangerous man.'

Burney was also sentenced to twelve years' imprisonment. Like Niven Craig, he had not long been released from a previous term, having been sent to penal servitude for five years for store-breaking and larceny in 1948. Before that, while serving in the Coldstream Guards, he had been sentenced to three years for desertion while in the forward area. On 31 October 1952, Niven Craig began his latest sentence in Wandsworth prison, a few miles from his parents' home in Norbury.

One question remained unanswered. The Craig parents had assumed that both Niven and Christopher were going off together to Norfolk for that February weekend of the Waltham Abbey robbery. In Niven's case, the jury dismissed the story. Where, then, was his younger brother on the night of the robbery? It was Christopher Craig's counsel, John Parris, who suggested that the fifteen-year-old might have been one of the other masked figures who confronted the Whitens that night.

On Friday 31 October, the conviction of Niven Craig and Cyril Burney was widely reported. But it was one story among several with a connecting theme. In the *News Chronicle* it appeared as BANDITS GET TWELVE YEARS, immediately under another report, MOTHERS SAY: FLOG THUGS. Nor was violence alone a cause for moral concern. Adjacent to these two features was a third: STOP THESE STAGE NUDES, HE SAYS. 'He' was George Tomlinson of the Public Morality Council. 'Parisian-style revues, specialising in "daring nude poses" were condemned yesterday for doing "incalculable harm to the large number of adolescents who patronise them."' By the Lord Chamberlain's ruling, nudity was only permitted on the English stage if the model remained immobile. The shows in question were apparently the Windmill Theatre's non-stop *Revuedeville*, where other girls danced in G-strings behind skilfully manipulated ostrich fans.

There was nothing new in this. The Windmill and its shows had been a boost to civilian and service morale during the war with a perky defiance of Hitler's blitz and a slogan 'We never closed.' The novelty by 1952 was in the new attitude towards such things. The morale-booster of wartime had become the danger to adolescent morality in the first decade of peace.

The *News Chronicle*, representing the Liberal centre of English politics, was restrained in its reporting of populist moral outrage, provoked by cases like that of Niven Craig. To the right, the *Daily Telegraph* accompanied its report of the trial with a story from Liverpool of a school petition: PARENTS WANT BIRCH RESTORED. More significantly, Lady Maxwell Fyfe, wife of the new Home Secretary, had taken up the cry. MOTHERS SHOULD USE THE BIRCH was her headlined message at Rhyl to the North Wales group of the Women Conservatives' Advisory Committee. But though the trial of Niven Craig added impetus to such moral sparring, the resolve to strike back at 'young thugs' had grown throughout the year. Lady Maxwell Fyfe readily lent her support, but the most vigorous and widely-reported advocacy for the reintroduction of flogging was that of Rayner Goddard, Lord Chief Justice of England.

By the autumn of 1952, the cosh-boys, thugs and young gunmen had become targets of an emotive and often hysterical response. In the popular press their role was much that of child abusers, child pornographers and rapists quarter of a century later. The source of the evil was seldom in doubt. Lack of parental control, dating back to the absence of fathers during the war, was part of it. Parents less willing to wield the birch than Lady Maxwell Fyfe had much to answer for.

The more clearly defined causes were comics, books, and films. BAN COMIC A WEEK FOR EVERY CHILD proclaimed the *Daily Telegraph* on 1 December, reporting the violence and evil example of comics for adolescents. On 4 December, the Home Secretary still declined to introduce an immediate law censoring comics. Parents must be the censors of their children's reading. ONLY FATHER CAN STOP BAD COMICS. But early in 1955 the importing and sale of crime comics and horror comics was prohibited by the Children and Young Persons (Harmful Publications) Act, a piece of legislation widely criticised in parliament and the press for its vagueness and irrelevance by then. Television, not comics, was to be the main source of juvenile entertainment. In 1952, however, American comics had been a feature of English childhood since the arrival of the first American servicemen during the war. Adult violence in comic-books had then been acceptable, even commendable, when its recipients were Germans and – especially – Japanese. But even America in the violent 1950s, under the newly-elected Eisenhower administration, was ill at ease. The day after the *Telegraph's* report, the *Daily Herald* added an account of a Congressional Committee in Washington – U.S. ATTACK ON DIRTY COMICS AND MAGAZINES – where sexual content was an equal issue with violence.

No less alarming, to the English press in 1952, was the availability of weapons. In the six weeks after the end of Niven Craig's case, weeks crucial to the fate of Christopher Craig and Derek Bentley, the headlines of the British press told a still more vivid story. STORE STOPS SELLING TOY TRUNCHEONS ... MP WAVES TOY COSH ... SCHOOLBOY ACCUSED OF GUN HOLD-UP ... GIRL STABBED ON BUS: SALESMAN SENTENCED TO DEATH ... CLOSING-TIME BANDITS COSH JEWELLER ... JUDGE TRIES ON KNUCKLE DUSTER ... FORTY-GUN CRAIG ... COSH-GIRL USES FIRE-TONGS ... BOY ARMED WITH STILETTO: WEAPONS' OPEN SALE ... 'JOIN MY COSH GANG,' SAID THE CHIEF, AGED 15 ... WHO HAS GUNS FOR SALE? NEW POLICE PROBE ... FIREARMS LAW MAY BE STRENGTHENED ...

There was a competing and yet complementary litany, which reported on 7 November that Scotland Yard had decided to employ civilian clerks in order to free desk-bound policemen to combat crime. On 12 December the courts were said to be jammed by a 'crime queue.' The truth was that the crime-rate had actually begun to fall and that violence against the person accounted for less than one and a half per cent of all crime in 1952.

9

Any mention of this was quickly dealt with. On 22 January 1953, in *The Times*, an advocate of flogging denounced the statistics of falling crime as getting in the way of 'general experience and general opinion.' He need not have worried. The headlines had already told the story that their readers feared and yet wanted to hear. WAVE OF CRIME 'A CHALLENGE', from the *Daily Telegraph* on 7 November. MORE ACTION DEMANDED TO MEET THE MENACE OF THE THUG: OLD FOLK ARE AFRAID TO GO TO BED, from the *Daily Herald* on 6 November. WOMEN GO IN FEAR AFTER DARK, from the same paper next day.

On the whole, it was the children of the poorer class who were seen as the stuff of which thugs and bullies were made. But not exclusively so. The malaise had spread everywhere. On 14 November, the *Daily Telegraph*, quoting an *Isis* editorial, revealed that the contamination had spread to Oxford undergraduates: OXFORD 'THUGS' CRITICISED. *Isis*, reporting the events of Guy Fawkes night, described the 'incomparable vulgarity' of the richer and idler young men who had knocked down a policeman, thrown a beer bottle through a bookseller's window and inflicted burns on a woman by throwing a firework at her. If the future leaders of England were infected by such contagion, what was to be done for the less privileged young?

The answer was in part to ban comics, books, and films likely to inflame the impulse to violence or, indeed, sexual desire. But there was one remedy, taken away by the law in 1948, for whose return the nation's moral leaders yearned. Its promise rang through columns of the press throughout November 1952. JPs MAY VOTE ON WHIPPING . . . BRING BACK BIRCH BILL IS COMING . . . JUDGE: IF I COULD ORDER BIRCH . . . PRO-BIRCH MEETING . . . TO FLOG OR NOT TO FLOG . . . ARCHDEACON SAYS: DON'T RULE OUT CORPORAL PUNISHMENT . . . 'CAT' DEMAND BY WOMEN . . . TOWN MEETING ASKS: BRING BACK CAT. From Sir Waldron Smithers, Sir Cyril Black and the burghers of Wimbledon, from the British Housewives League, from the Conservative Women's Advisory Committee, from magistrates and civic leaders, the message was unambiguous.

Occasionally during these six weeks there was a discordant note. The *Daily Herald* in its editorial of 4 November was tactless enough to mention that the crimes for which flogging was prescribed in the old days were actually decreasing in number. On 4 December, there were several reports of the latest conviction of an offender who was first sentenced to flogging when he was twelve and was still coming before the courts, undeterred, at the age of fifty. On the same day it was reported that the workshops at Dartmoor had been burnt down by prisoners in protest against the flogging of a convict, still permitted by the law. On 11 December a fear of prison mutiny was added to this.

Worst of all was the revelation by an approved school headmaster, J. D. Johnson, of the 'Birching Farce'. Incomprehensible though it might be to the moral vigilantes, he explained that many policemen did not actually like birching young offenders. He had witnessed scenes of officers passing the birch from hand to hand, each one unwilling to use it. Other men and women were more resolute. Sentencing two youths on 17 November, the Recorder of Southend (reported next day in the *News Chronicle*), regretted wistfully that he could not birch them 'firmly and steadily,' as he rather curiously put it.

At first the outbursts and musings of the moral vigilantes appeared absurd rather than sinister. To a generation born after Freud and Krafft-Ebing, the middle-aged enthusiasm of the Conservative Women's Advisory Committee for wielding the birch on young men was inseparable from sexual innuendo. Had the proposed law made democratic provision for the Conservative ladies to be equally subject to its provision, a healthy doubt might speedily have been sown among them. Penalties prescribed by the law must be democratically and universally applicable. Even as matters stood, correspondents suggested that female criminals of the 'Cosh-girl uses fire-tongs' breed should suffer the same penalty as their male contemporaries. Why should the middle-aged or the stalwarts of the Conservative Women be immune from the law? Violence suffered from their arrogance at the wheel of a car or in their treatment of elderly relatives was sometimes worse than that endured by the victims of the cosh. That surely ought not to be overlooked. It was at this stage of the argument that the predilections of the vigilantes showed them for what they were. They belonged to a rank which should exempt them from such provisions. There was another level of lesser breeds to whom the provision must apply.

Misrepresentation and farce may be the stuff of newspaper profits at such times of public anxiety. But though the crime-rate might be falling and the proposed remedies suspect, this was of little comfort to those who woke in the night with a torch in their faces and masked figures round their bed. Nor was it of comfort to those who read the newspapers and lived in fear of such things. Scapegoats were sought. Comics, novels, films, and stage nudity, even parental irresponsibility would do to be going on with. But far more effective than such ill-defined causes was a flesh and blood example. His fate would warm the hearts of the righteous and cool the enthusiasm of the young thugs, cosh-boys, gunmen and bullies.

If the press could be believed, the nation had never been more in the mood to strike back at its public enemies than it was in the early autumn of 1952.

CHAPTER 2

On 18 October 1952, even before Niven Craig's appearance in the dock at the Old Bailey, armed robbery came to Croydon for the first but not the last time that autumn. It was later said that sixteen-year-old Christopher Craig's hatred of the police and his dedication to crime were the result of seeing his idolised elder brother sent to prison for twelve years. According to one of his former schoolfriends, quoted at the time in the *Daily Telegraph*, the effect of Niven Craig's fate on Christopher was 'to finish him completely'. But almost two weeks before that he was already 'finished,' in the sense of having chosen crime as the means of rebellion. The armed robbery of 18 October was the younger Craig's idea. He carried it out with the aid of Norman Parsley, a bright grammar school boy with a place waiting for him at university. The age of both masked gunmen was just sixteen.

The social background of the two criminals seemed as improbable as the scene of the crime. Moreover, it could hardly have happened to a nicer place, or one with more cherished middle-class pretensions. In the last years of peace before 1939, no less than after 1945, the ambitions of many Londoners were directed southward as well as upward. East Croydon station, fifteen minutes or so by electric train from the centre of the capital, brought them to another world of suburban affluence, where the breath of the sea at Brighton seemed almost to be in the air. Before them lay the green hills of Purley and Coulsdon, still leafy despite the climbing avenues of modernistic white villas with their crisp architectural lines behind hedges of laurel and yew. A new semi-detached 'weatherproof' house in the quiet avenues of Coulsdon could be bought just before the war for £625. A full-time servant to ease the burden of domestic chores could be hired for £1 a week. All this might be enjoyed within sight of green hills and woods but with the grimy commercial centre of London no more than half an hour away by electric rail. And when the time came to hang up the bowler hat and the umbrella, to retire to the seaside, Andereida Ltd offered new architect-designed homes at Pevensey Bay from £325.

It was too good to last, or at any rate to survive a world war. After 1945, servants were hard to find at any price. Work in shops and factories brought greater freedom as well as more money. But the white houses of Coulsdon and Purley, the hillside avenues and the green distances of Surrey remained.

1945 had signalled a second exodus, this time from the poorer boroughs of central London, where demolition contractors were completing the destruction that the Luftwaffe had begun. A second wave of emigrants, less affluent but equally ambitious, began to fill the streets of Norbury and Streatham, immediately to the north of Croydon. The earlier arrivals reacted with the displeasure felt by those settlers who win their place in prosperity, only to find a larger and rougher influx close on their heels. The very people and problems they had left behind for ever were now encroaching from the north.

Croydon was divided at its High Street shopping centre, South End running out to the green hills and North End leading into the London Road and the long streets of sooty Victorian brick. In the busy and affluent centre, the style was set by the white angular modernism of Kennard's department store, whose publicity included Riviera Bathing Parades and visits by film stars.

Between Croydon and Streatham lay close-packed residential areas of south London which had been battered by the wartime blitz and particularly by the V-2 rocket attacks of 1944, when the southern part of the capital had been more clearly a target. In the new age of peace, Norbury and Thornton Heath looked for their pleasures either north to Streatham with its Ice Rink and Astoria or, more often, south to Croydon with its numerous cinemas, its dancing at the Lido, and its own Purley Ice Rink.

The Craig family lived in one of the better residential avenues off the long arterial London Road which ran northwards, under various names, ten miles or so from the centre of Croydon to Westminster Bridge. Apart from Niven Craig, the older children had made a success of their lives. The parents were respected in the neighbourhood. Mr Craig had risen to be cashier of a bank in Victoria Street, to which he commuted daily from Norbury station. Mrs Craig was a gentle and intelligent woman who had once broadcast, during the war for the BBC, on the problems of juvenile delinquency.

On 18 October, Christopher Craig was in company with Norman Parsley. It was a Saturday and, in its way, quite as boring as most Sundays proved to be. According to Parsley's later account, Craig said, 'I've got something on tonight. There's no risk.'

'Something' was to be an armed raid on a house in South Croydon, occupied by Christopher Howes, an elderly green-grocer who lived there with his wife. After Mr Howes had cashed up and gone home with the takings, the money would be in the house over the weekend, waiting to be snatched. That at least was the plan. Norman Parsley seems not to have cared greatly either way but it was worth a try. As Craig described the prospects, there might be some rich pickings. 'I had nothing to do and was fed up, browned off,' Parsley said, 'and I agreed to go with him.'

They caught a bus from Norbury along two or three miles of the shabby arterial road to the greener pastures of South Croydon. Mr Howes and his wife lived in Avon Path, to the east of the Brighton Road and almost adjacent to the playing fields of Archbishop Whitgift's school. As at Waltham Forest, this was to be a robbery in disguise. Even so, Norman Parsley's account of the preparations made the whole thing sound more like a schoolboy prank than the act of desperate criminals. 'I was wearing my dad's trilby and I had a white scarf over my face.' As they approached the house, Craig handed him 'a black gun with a shiny barrel'. Craig himself was carrying a second gun, probably an Eley .455 revolver with a sawn-off barrel. 'We agreed not to use the guns unless we had to,' Parsley told the police. The gun Craig handed him seems likely to have been a .22, since this was the type of weapon he was most often seen with.

'It's easy,' Craig said, 'All we have to do is to walk up to the door, knock, and then we're in.'

That, at least, was part of the plan that worked. Mrs Howes answered the door and screamed at the sight of the two masked figures in their long coats and trilby hats. They pushed her inside. She either fell or was pushed to the ground. Mr Howes appeared, to be confronted by the sight of the door closed again and two gunmen facing him. His wife was by then writhing and moaning on the floor.

Like a good many people in October 1952, Mr Howes may have been scared by the thought of 'rising crime' and 'gunmen'. But also, like a good many, he held such criminals in angry contempt.

'Give us your wallet,' Craig said.

Mr Howes did not hand over his wallet. Instead, he said, 'There's nothing in it.'

In response to the threat of the guns, he indicated a pile of receipts. 'Look, I've just paid bills for £71. I've no money.'

It seemed like stalemate, which was not how an armed robbery was supposed to be. Mr Howes picked up a bag of loose change from the sideboard. 'Here,' he said, 'Take this and get out.'

Mrs Howes was now on her feet again. Speedily recovered from her fall and her shock, she brushed the guns aside, saying, 'They're toys!' Then she tried to snatch the scarf from Parsley's face. Craig displayed the bullets in his revolver and said in his practised gangster drawl, 'Take a look at these, lady.'

Stalemate again.

'Get in the sitting-room,' Craig said, 'We're going to tie you up.'

The elderly Mr Howes was unimpressed. A generation that had seen off Adolf Hitler and the military power of the Third Reich was not going to cave in when confronted by a pair of bullying adolescents.

'That's not necessary,' he said firmly, 'Get off these premises.'

And, quite contrary to the horror stories of the popular press, the two masked gunmen did as they were told. Their haul was about £4 in silver coins. Craig gave half of it to Parsley. They caught a northbound bus and went to the cinema at the Streatham

Astoria. After that they went home.

The armed robbery in Avon Path was something less than the stuff of which the Bogart and Cagney legend had been made. Dream turned to reality and the two gangsters, spoken to sharply, behaved like the unruly children they still were. Norman Parsley returned his father's trilby hat to its place. No one at that time had reason to suspect either of the boys, whose identity had been concealed. Perhaps someone in the Metropolitan Police might have reflected that the style of the disguises and the proposed tying up of the victims while the house was ransacked woke echoes of the robbery at Waltham Abbey. But then, the brains behind that particular crime were assumed to be on remand in Brixton prison.

A truly professional criminal would have run for his life in the opposite direction to either of the Craig brothers, or Norman Parsley or Ginger King. Their level of criminal competence had less in common with the legend of the Hollywood gunman than with its great contemporary rival on the cinema screens of England, the Ealing Studios Comedy. This was not to say that they were harmless. Precisely because they were amateur and easily nonplussed, they were far more dangerous. In the presence of the elderly greengrocer and his wife, their bluff was called. Craig and Parsley could either shoot or give up. On this occasion they gave up. It required only a change of mood, a surge of resentment, for Craig to shoot instead.

To have taken such risks for such paltry rewards would appear to be absurd. The proceeds of the Waltham Forest robbery worked out at less than £1 a head for those who had taken part. Their eventual reward was twelve years penal servitude. The shares from the Croydon armed robbery were less than an afternoon's work by an apprentice shoplifter. The penalty would have been infinitely greater. Four years imprisonment in the case of Parsley. He was to be caught, after all, for a reason no one could have foreseen.

The true professional might have dismissed such escapades as the antics of a group of incompetent clowns. Behind the grand phrase 'armed robbery,' with its associations of armoured trucks or steel doors blown open and gun battles raging all about, there was after all only the aggressive adolescent whine.

'Give us your wallet!'

But failure and frustration bred a bitterness that knew no limits. The amateur gunman failed, time and again, to make his mark. At last the 'need' to use a gun as the last resort became an eagerness to use it at the first opportunity. In that lay the true peril.

CHAPTER 3

On a dry, dull Sunday in the fall of the year, the close-packed house-roofs and empty streets of south London symbolised tedium and inertia to the first adolescent generation of the 1950s. They were less prone to tolerate domestic boredom than their compliant forebears of the 1930s. In a decade when the family Sunday remained sacred to secular rituals of tabloid-reading and television viewing, the sabbath proprieties of the middle-aged oppressed the impatient young. Some grew as openly contemptuous as they were of their parents' nostalgia for the Finest Hour and the Dunkirk Spirit. Such young people were known rather warily, for the first time, as 'teenagers.' Educationalists thought them an interesting and sympathetic cultural novelty. Families found them difficult. Under the dull November sky that stretched from Lambeth to Purley, the Sunday afternoon world was dead to them except where the plaques of red and green neon shimmered with a promise of glamour and excitement over the glass doors of cinemas in Streatham, Norbury, or Croydon.

My Death is a Mockery was the film to which Christopher Craig took his girl-friend on that particular afternoon, 2 November 1952, a fortnight after the robbery in South Croydon and three days after his elder brother's trial. The police had no reason yet to connect him or Norman Parsley with Mr Howes' description of the two masked and trilby-hatted gunmen.

At sixteen, Christopher Craig was just old enough to be admitted to gangster films with their 'Adult' certificates and to Sunday performances. With much of the British film industry in the hands of the Methodist flour-miller, J. Arthur Rank, the object of a minimum age on Sunday was to ensure that the young were not lured to the cinema when they might have been at church or

Sunday school. That lure was real enough, and by the evening performances there were long queues for seats. The cinema was still the favoured escape of the post-war young, cocooning its audiences in living dreams of American affluence or heroic melodrama.

Sunday afternoon in the miles of South London residential streets from Lambeth to Croydon was also the time for a parade of adolescent fashion and possession. The boys appeared with hair slickly waved and combed in a 'duck's arse,' or else worn long with sideburns in Teddy Boy fashion. Their narrow trousers and long jackets were sharply tailored. This appearance was complemented by the girls in their full pleated skirts and tight jumpers. 'Putting on the agony, putting on the style,' as the song described it, the teenagers of the shabby streets began their afternoon migration to a hundred Odeons and Regals, Gaumonts and ABCs, or to the cafés where Italian espresso coffee and the hiss of its machinery were a fashionable novelty.

Christopher Craig went to the cinema three or four times a week, to gangster films for preference. His taste was no different in that respect from thousands of his contemporaries. Nor did the moral message of this film vary from the rule. *My Death is a Mockery* mingled crime and morality in a manner that the Victorians or the Middle Ages might have recognised, when employed by Charles Dickens in *Oliver Twist* or by Geoffrey Chaucer in *The Pardoner's Tale*. It was a British-made film, a contemporary tale of smuggling and of a man who killed a French policeman and was hanged for his crime.

In all the head-shaking over the evil influence of the cinema, it was apt to be forgotten that no film could get on to the British screen without having satisfied the British Board of Film Censors and, in the case of transatlantic imports, the even stricter conditions of the so-called Hays Code in the United States. Despite the occasional lurid title, the message of the crime film was at one with evangelical morality. 'Be sure your sins will find you out,' or 'They that live by the sword shall perish by the sword,' characterised screen ethics and pulpit alike.

The 1950s shared with the 1980s an easy assumption that the ills of society could be blamed on the 'violence' and 'sex' of books, films, or television. It was a quick and easy explanation, being provable either way, according to taste and dogma. It also short-circuited the need to look for more politically embarrassing explanations. In the wake of the Craig and Bentley case, the title of *My Death is a Mockery* was to be quoted, as if the screenplay was a direct incitement to teenage gunmen. But *My Death is a Mockery* was very far from the hard-boiled gangsterdom of George Raft and Humphrey Bogart. It starred the mild and reassuring faces of Donald Houston and Bill Kerr. Both were better known for comedy, Houston was probably best known as the Welsh medical student in *Doctor in the House*, while Bill Kerr was to become a household name for his role in the broadcasts of *Hancock's Half Hour*.

All the same, Craig sat through the film with the loaded .455 Eley service revolver in his coat. At the garage where he worked, he had access to the tools necessary to shorten the barrel so that the gun would fit into his pocket.

He left the cinema in the early November dusk and went home to tea. With his parents and their younger children he lived in a tree-lined avenue, Norbury Court Road. There were eight sons and daughters, Christopher being the youngest of all. Norbury Court Road was one of innumerable turnings leading off the long arterial drabness of the main route from Croydon through Thornton Heath, Streatham, Brixton, to Lambeth and the Thames at Westminster.

In many respects, the Craig household belonged to a world of steady prosperity and middle-class aspiration. The boy's father, now a bank cashier, had served with distinction as an army captain in the First World War, and in the Home Guard during Hitler's war. He had made a name for himself as an amateur sportsman in rugger and boxing, turning later to pigeon-racing and becoming a member of the Appeals Committee of the London Pigeon Parliament.

One of the many ironies in the case was that the Craig and Bentley families, in different ways, gave precisely the care and affection to their children which the anxious moralists were now demanding. There was nothing of the broken home or parental indifference. Christopher Craig had been sent to Bible class regularly at a Streatham church until he was thirteen or fourteen. He gave this up on the pretext that he was afraid of being asked to read a lesson and not being able to do it because of his 'word blindness.' It was also this which prevented his receiving a grammar school education, something which Mr Craig paid for in the case of his other children.

With two exceptions, the Craig children had done well. Acquaintances who heard the stories of Niven and Christopher were apt to feel that their parents did not deserve such sons as these. But their father retained an attachment to his military past and an interest in firearms, even to the extent of being fined for possessing a gun without a licence during the Second World War. Indeed, as a serving officer, Captain Craig had been rated the fourth best shot in the British Army. When the two boys were old enough, he had taught both Niven and Christopher to shoot. But even after the elder son's convictions, he did not know that sixteen-year-old Christopher had possessed between forty and fifty guns of his own from time to time, taking them to school, showing them to his friends, and swapping them for other weapons. It has to be said that most of them seem to have been trophies and no more. Of the forty or fifty guns, he had only been able to fire about ten. All the same, he had a secret store of ammunition hidden in a tin under the attic floorboards, as well as a long-bladed sheath-knife which he wore on his belt, and a couple of knuckledusters.

Though there was much synchronised dismay in the press and in public debate at the secret armoury of the young Craig, the truth was that youthful ownership of such trophies was more widespread than the press admitted or the public knew. Knives of this kind were cultivated and firearms swapped among adolescent boys in fee-paying public schools as well as among their less privileged contemporaries in Norbury Manor Secondary Modern. Though against the rules, ownership of air-pistols among the future leaders of the nation at public schools was not unknown and even the possession of more powerful firearms was not beyond adolescent ingenuity. As for the bullets, most of the ammunition in Craig's bedroom had been picked up at Coulsdon from the open ground of the rifle range at Caterham Barracks. Among other boys, younger than he, the same cartridges were traded innocently as 'souvenirs'. Craig's distinction, at sixteen, was that he had already begun to use weapons and ammunition in his first criminal enterprises.

Craig's Eley .455 came from Purley. When it was suggested that he had stolen it from a house there at the beginning of 1952, he denied this. He insisted that he had got it from a friend, Martin Vincent, who lived in the area. Even so it was stolen, but the owner had no licence for the gun and so chose not to report the theft to the police. Like other teenagers of the day, Christopher Craig acquired guns that were merely souvenirs in themselves and then found ways of making them work with improvised ammunition. 'I had one gun,' he recalled, 'I used to put a .22 in and a blank, and fire that, and it went like an air-gun. It made a bit of a bang and you could fire it.' You could, of course, also kill someone with it.

In the autumn of 1951, he had run away from home with another boy and had subsequently been fined by a juvenile court at Hove for illegal possession of a .45 Webley revolver. Apart from this, he had no criminal record. The pair of fugitives had been hiding under a boat on the beach, hoping to cross to France, dreaming of adventure. Had Craig's future been blander, the entire escapade might easily have been written off as adolescent bravado.

Though he and nineteen-year-old Derek Bentley were subsequently credited with a number of break-ins during the summer of 1952, the only joint suspicion to fall on them before November was in connection with some stolen petrol. No case was proved or even brought against them. Before that autumn Sunday of *My Death is a Mockery*, neither Craig nor Bentley appeared to be the stuff of which famous criminals are made. Despite what the *Daily Mirror* called his 'film tough-guy drawl,' those who encountered Christopher Craig were apt to be unimpressed by him. They found him moody and depressed since leaving school. He was intelligent but almost illiterate, able to make his way through children's comics or junior school reading primers but otherwise relying on his parents and older sisters to read aloud to him in the evenings.

One of the more bizarre revelations was that the ruthless teenage gunman was still in the habit of being read aloud to at home, his choice governed by what his family could be persuaded to read to him. So it was not Craig but the unoffending middle-class bookworm whose thrills came from the sado-sexual antics of Mickey Spillane's heroes or the villains of James Hadley Chase. To Christopher Craig, as to Derek Bentley, such novels were literally a closed book.

According to Derek Bentley's father, William Bentley, Craig had called for his son on the previous evening, Saturday 1 November. Derek was out, at the cinema. Craig proudly showed the younger Bentley son, Denis, a knuckleduster that he had made at the garage where he worked. It was later to be produced at his trial, worn and displayed at the Old Bailey by the Lord Chief Justice.

'You put it on your hand to knock a man down,' Craig explained to Denis Bentley, 'When you've got him on the floor, you hit him with this.'

'This' was a savage spike that protruded to one side of the knuckleduster and could be used as a dagger with the force of a clenched fist behind it. When Mrs Bentley appeared he showed her the weapon and explained that it was better than those that could be bought. She recalled that she told him it was stupid to carry such a thing about and advised him to throw it away. If the police caught him with it, she added, he would be in serious trouble. According to Mrs Bentley, Craig said, 'A fat lot I care for the police. They're a lot of bloody fools.'

Again she advised him to get rid of it and suggested that his own mother would tell him the same. The answer that Craig gave her was thought to explain a good deal about his conduct on the following day.

'We don't like the police – see! They've just given my brother, Niven, twelve years. Do you think I'm going to let them get away with that? I'm going to get my own back some day – and how!'

Mrs Bentley repeated her advice again. But the boy ran off, shouting, 'They'll never take me alive!'

Such evidence offered by the Bentley parents was part of an attempt to show that their simple-minded son had been the dupe and Craig the evil genius. It was not to be expected that they would be impartial. But Derek Bentley himself, in his statement to the police, admitted that his parents had tried to prevent him seeing Craig in the past few months. And Craig's own words on the following evening, recorded at his trial, confirm his state of mind as Mrs Bentley described it.

Craig had come back next morning just before lunch. According to Mr Bentley, the two youths were talking at the front door. The Bentleys' younger son Denis was close by.

'Come out. I want to talk to you,' Craig said to Derek Bentley.

Bentley refused. Then Craig saw Denis Bentley and said, 'Send that kid away. I've got something to say to you.'

But the child remained close enough to hear Bentley's reply to whatever Craig had to say.

'I don't want anything to do with it. Leave me alone.'

Denis went and told his father. Mr Bentley confronted Derek after Craig had gone. He demanded an explanation. His son would only say, 'It's nothing, Dad, it's nothing. The bloke's barmy.'

William Bentley was not reassured. He later claimed that he had been to Norbury police station on the previous Monday and had asked Sergeant Reed for some protection of his son against Craig and his influence. But there was nothing that the police or the law could do to help him.

On that Sunday of 2 November, Craig went home from the cinema and ate a meal. At about 8.30 in the evening, he walked a few streets north from his home to Fairview Road, opposite Norbury railway station on the main London Road. He was wearing his long coat and trilby hat, his corduroy jacket in tribute to his brother 'The Velvet Kid,' and the slim-legged drainpipe trousers of male fashion. Added to the soft immaturity of his appearance, the costume appeared absurd rather than menacing.

But he had his sheath-knife in his belt and carried his knuckleduster. In the pocket of his coat lay the .455 Eley revolver with its sawn-off barrel.

By this time on a Sunday evening, teenage groups had begun to gather on the corners of London Road. Opposite the station, outside the newsagent and tobacconist, Craig met Norman Parsley and Frank Fazey.

There was no sign of Derek Bentley, the elder by three years of the group that gathered outside the newsagent's shop. To Craig, this was a matter of some importance. The reason he subsequently gave for going round to see Bentley that evening contradicted William Bentley's story of a son who wanted nothing to do with Craig. On the previous day, in Tamworth Road, West Croydon, Derek Bentley had picked up the keys to a butcher's shop while no one was watching him. He had 'dared' Craig to come with him and rob the shop that Sunday night. If the week-end takings had been left on the premises to be banked on Monday, then the 'result' would be the best and easiest so far. Craig walked into the side-turning of Fairview Road and rang the doorbell of the first house. Mrs Bentley appeared, took one look at Craig, and told him that her son was out.

This was untrue. Derek Bentley was watching television in the sitting room but his mother had no intention of enabling him to go out that Sunday evening in Craig's company. Bentley had also been to the cinema that afternoon, returning home at about seven o'clock. His choice had been less sensational than Craig's. He had been to the Streatham Astoria, where his sister worked as an usherette and where the film was *The Lady from the West*, starring Betty Grable. He had arrived after the beginning of the film and left early with a headache. Given the quality of some film-projection at that date, a headache after going to the cinema was not an uncommon experience.

Mrs Bentley and her husband had particular reason to feel uneasy about the company that their son kept. Though tall, physically well-developed and older than the street corner group, Derek Bentley was close to being feeble-minded. He was effectively illiterate, with a reading age of a child of four and a half. He could not spell his own Christian name when he signed a statement nor read the oath when giving evidence. His IQ was sixty-six and his mental age was put at somewhere between ten and eleven years old. He had suffered from epilepsy and from head injuries when the family home was bombed during the war. A history of family ill-health was suggested by the early death of a brother who had been born a mongol.

Derek Bentley had been a petty and unsuccessful thief, though not an habitual one. After appearing before Croydon magistrates for a second time at the age of fifteen, he had spent almost two years at Kingswood Approved School, near Bristol, and had been treated at the Burden Neurological Institute nearby. His family background and career were less prepossessing than those of Craig. His father had been given a job as an engineer with the South-East Electricity Board, when he was demobbed from the army in 1946, and had set up a small repair shop in his home. The years after the war had seen some improvement in the prospects of the Bentley family, who had moved south from Walworth. But there were few middle-class pretensions in Fairview Road, where Derek Bentley at nineteen still shared a bedroom with his Uncle Albert. The window at the foot of his bed looked out, appropriately enough, on to a tumble of South London back yards, a garage park, distant blank walls and bare winter trees.

After the end of his education at fifteen and his release from the approved school, he had worked for Albert Hutchins, a friend of his father's who was a furniture remover. When that job ended because he strained his back, he was employed as a dustman by Croydon Corporation. When that seemed beyond him, he was downgraded to road-sweeper. By November 1952 he was unemployed, and possibly unemployable. Those who believed that two years' National Service in the army would work wonders with society's misfits were to be disappointed in this case. On 11 February 1952, he went for his National Service medical. He was certified as being subject to *petit mal* and was found to be 'mentally sub-standard.' He was put in Grade IV and classified as unfit for military service.

In appearance, at least, he seemed to typify his generation and class. The long jacket and drainpipe trousers, the brightly-patterned shirt and carefully waved fair hair were as much a uniform as the battledress of the army which rejected him. He had taken up body-building to improve his appearance but, like so many of his contemporaries, the clothes made the man.

Unaware that it was Craig at the door, Bentley sat in front of the family television set watching a programme of old-time music-hall. The keys to the butcher's shop might be in his pocket, but he was all dressed up and nowhere as yet to go.

Craig went back to the street corner. Without the stolen keys, there was little point to the evening's expedition. After a short interval, the doorbell at the house in Fairview Road rang again. This time Mrs Bentley was confronted by Norman Parsley and Frank Fazey, two well-spoken grammar-school boys, about whom she knew nothing discreditable. Though she did not invite them in, she went to the sitting room and told her son the names of the two boys who had called. Derek Bentley got up from his chair and went out into the street after them. It was then that he saw Craig, who was waiting with the others by the corner newsagent's shop.

It was now almost nine o'clock. Craig and Bentley left the other two boys and crossed the road to catch the 109 bus to West Croydon suburban railway station, a mile or so to the south on the arterial London Road. Both were now dressed in the coats and trilby hats that made an easy disguise. There were few passengers to Croydon at this time on a Sunday evening. As they sat together, Craig handed Bentley the home-made knuckleduster that he had shown to Mrs Bentley the day before.

By comparison with Craig, Bentley seemed lightly armed. It was to be said in his defence that he had no record of violence. He had a sheath-knife in his coat pocket and the knuckleduster just given to him. But at this stage of the evening, there seemed no occasion for the weapons except as totems. The two teenagers carried them now as Craig carried them when he went to school. Off London Road, Croydon, they expected to find the butcher's shop empty and waiting to be unlocked by the stolen keys. Guns, knives and knuckledusters were no part of the plan.

Yet the memorial of two violent deaths, including Bentley's, was already close at hand. As the bus lumbered its way towards West Croydon station, a dark space appeared among the little shops and streets of Thornton Heath. It was the edge of Mitcham Common and the cemetery where he and the man for whose murder he was hanged were eventually to lie. Beyond it, the shabbier approach to Croydon began on the long London Road. There was the ABC Savoy cinema, the detached Victorian houses occupied by insurance offices, the Broad Green Independent Grammar School whose smartly uniformed adolescent girls turned the heads of the new generation.

West Croydon station, where Craig and Bentley got off the bus, was some way short of the shopping-centre intersection that marked the heart of the prospering town. Craig and Bentley crossed London Road to the toilets and telephone box at the corner of Tamworth Road. Tamworth Road was a thoroughfare of sooty brick, a mixture of houses, shops, storage, and the Robert Peel public house, connecting London Road and Church Street. Its bleak urban landscape ended in the west with drifts of smoke from the squat cooling towers of Croydon power station. The two hopeful thieves in their long coats and trilby hats stopped outside the butcher's shop. There was a light on above the door and sounds of movement inside the shop. They waited for a while on the other side of the road to see if whoever was in the shop might leave. No one did.

Uncertain who was there, or how many people, Craig and Bentley walked on, looking for an opportunity elsewhere. The last time Craig had tried to rob occupied premises, the result had been a fiasco. In any case, it was one thing to confront an elderly greengrocer and his wife in South Croydon but the butcher's shop was now an unknown quantity. There was an electrical shop down the road, and that seemed promising, until they noticed a courting couple standing together in its shadows. There was nothing for it but to move on again. It was not the goods in a shop that were the immediate attraction but the prospect of cash left unbanked over the weekend.

They came to the next road junction, a saleroom of secondhand goods known as Reeves' Corner. There was a pause. Then they crossed over and came back along the other pavement of Tamworth Road, stopping at last outside Barlow and Parker's confectionery warehouse. This building, the largest commercial premises among the houses of the street, was in darkness. Craig had heard that a good deal of money was left there over the weekend, if only one could get at it. He tried to peer through the window and Bentley attempted to open the double gates, but these were securely locked. The best hope for a break-in was to scale the wall and then either force the door on the flat roof or else smash open one of the glass roof-lights. The only way in, to begin with, was to climb a high iron-spiked gate at the side, leading to a narrow passageway along one wall of the building.

CHAPTER 4

Tamworth Road was deserted at this time on a Sunday evening, though a bus route ran along it. It is a measure of their ineptitude that the two aspiring thieves did almost everything in their power to advertise their presence and their intentions. Every time a bus or car passed by, they pulled their hats down and looked furtive. They made a good deal of noise by trying to open the main double doors of the yard and, later, by Bentley walking into a dustbin. Set against the standards of *Rififi*, it was something less than a professional performance.

Once out of the street lighting, however, they would not easily be seen. The night was cloudy, though dry, with what was afterwards described as only a fitful moonlight. At last Craig took the initiative, clambering up the side gate, over the spikes at the top, and down into the passageway that ran along the side of the warehouse. Bentley followed him, finding some difficulty in getting over the six-foot gate. Apart from being encumbered rather than assisted by Bentley, Craig was already in more trouble than he realised. Despite the pulling down of hats and other attempts at concealment, the two burglars had ignored the lighted windows of the houses across the road and the possibility that someone living there might see them at work.

Still in their long coats and hats, they began to climb the drainpipes that led to the flat roof from the passageway in which they had been standing. Craig got up to the low parapet-wall with its two-foot guard-rail and pulled himself on to the roof. Bentley, whose physical co-ordination was poor, chose a separate pipe and got stuck. He came back down again and tried the way that Craig had chosen. 'I went on Craig's drainpipe and got up,' he explained later.

On the opposite side of the street, at 74 Tamworth Road, Mrs Edith Ware stood back from her daughter's bedroom window. The nine-year-old, whose observation was soon to be rewarded by having her picture in the national press, had drawn her mother's attention to the two men on the opposite pavement. Even a child could see them for what they were. Short of wearing a Bill Sikes costume, they could hardly have been more conspicuous. 'When I saw them climbing over,' the child told the press proudly, 'I shouted to my Mum and Dad, and Dad ran out to dial 999.'

'They were just standing there talking for a few minutes and pulling their hats over their eyes,' said Mrs Ware, 'Every time a bus came along they pulled their hats down and stood talking. And then all of a sudden the shorter one of the two jumped right over the fence at the side on the left.'

Mrs Ware watched as Bentley hesitated. A car came round the corner. When it had gone and the road seemed deserted again, Bentley followed Craig over the gate. Mrs Ware went out of the room and told her husband. It was then just after 9.15. Mr Ware was shaving.

'Fetch the police, Jack,' she said, describing what she had seen.

There was no phone in the house. Mr Ware wiped the lather off his face, changed his slippers for shoes and went out into the street. He walked casually to the phone-box at the end of the road, knowing that he would draw the suspects' attention if he ran. The box was about fifty yards from the house. Reaching it without attracting notice, he dialled 999.

Croydon police station, next to the town hall, was within a stone's throw of the cross-roads at the town centre and about a quarter of a mile from Tamworth Road. Detective-Constable Frederick Fairfax had just parked his car in the police station yard and settled down to write a report on a gas-meter theft, when the message came in. 'Suspects on premises, Barlow and Parker, Tamworth Road.' He went out to the yard and met PC Norman Harrison who was on his way to the canteen before going on watch. With PC Pain and PC Budgen, the two men got into a police van and set off for Tamworth Road. Fairfax was in plain clothes and the other three in uniform. They were there within about four minutes of the telephone call. But the alarm had also been picked up by a wireless car, 7Z, on patrol in London Road. It was driven by PC Sidney Miles with PC James McDonald as his radio operator. The car arrived at Barlow and Parker's warehouse a few minutes after the van.

By this time, both Craig and Bentley were on the flat roof. They were twenty-two feet above the ground and had taken stock of their surroundings. The half of the roof further from Tamworth Road was the scene of the events which followed. It was about forty feet square. At its centre were four glass roof-lights, each sloping up to a height of four and a half feet above the roof itself. At the rear of the roof was a brick stack, the head of the lift-shaft, eleven and a half feet high. At the forward left-hand corner of that rear half, at right angles to the lift shaft and about forty feet from it, the door at the head of the interior staircase opened on to the roof. Below lay the yards and loading bay of Barlow and Parker, and the gardens of surrounding houses. A guard-rail, about two feet high, ran round the edge of the roof above the low parapet wall.

The first indication that something was wrong with their plan was when Bentley saw a torch shining up from one of the adjoining gardens and heard the sound of voices. Someone called out to them. By now they were standing close to the stack, the head of the lift-shaft, as far back from Tamworth Road and its street lights as they could get. There was a clatter of someone climbing up the drainpipe.

'It's a copper. Get behind here,' Craig said, moving to the stack. Bentley followed as he was told.

Until this point, according to Bentley, he did not know whether or not they would break into the building. His accusers insisted that he must have intended it. But it seems far more likely that the climb to the roof was a reconnaissance, opportunism rather than fixed intention. The butcher's shop had been no good. Nor the electrical goods shop. They would try their luck here instead. If it failed them, they could climb down and move on elsewhere. Given his mental ability and outlook, hard and fast planning was not Bentley's way of doing things.

Far more important in a few hours more, Bentley insisted that he did not know as they hid behind the stack that Craig was carrying a gun. This was later taken as if Bentley was sure in his own mind that Craig was not carrying a gun. In that case, to judge by his own words at the height of the action, Bentley was a liar. But the truth is more likely to be that Bentley did not know about the gun, in the sense that he did not know whether Craig was carrying it or not. It was none of his business and he might not have asked or even thought about it. Since the plan for that night had always been to break into an empty building, the gun was scarcely relevant.

PC Miles set off to find the key-holder, so that the police could enter the building. It was Fairfax who meanwhile made his way to the roof. Despite his civilian suit, Detective-Constable Fairfax looked like a policeman of the 1950s. Perhaps it was just that his dark-haired and balding appearance had a certain resemblance to the film actor Bruce Seton, well-known at the time for his Scotland Yard portrayals.

Fairfax followed the same route as the intruders. He climbed over the side-gate with its iron spikes, walked down the passageway at the side of the warehouse and found the drainpipe by which the suspects had got to the roof. 'There was not much room,' he recalled, 'and so away from street lights visibility was bad.' He clambered up and came on to the side of the asphalt roof near the well-head of the staircase, about forty feet diagonally from the brick stack of the lift-shaft. He had no torch but he could see Craig and Bentley, who were now between him and the stack. They were standing beyond the glass roof-lights, about thirty feet from him.

As Fairfax walked towards them, they backed away behind the stack again. There was a narrow path between the back of the stack and the edge of the roof, protected by the guard-rail and parapet wall at the roof's rear edge.

'I am a police officer,' Fairfax shouted, 'Come out from behind that stack!'

Craig gave the reply.

'If you want us, fucking well come and get us!'

'All right,' Fairfax said, rushing at the stack behind which the two fugitives were wedged on the narrow path. Bentley was nearer to him. Fairfax grabbed hold of Bentley by the left arm and began to advance on Craig, pushing Bentley at the same time.

'I am a police officer,' Fairfax said as he clutched Bentley, 'The place is surrounded.'

This was the point at which the pair of adolescent thieves would usually decide that the game was up or that it was a fair cop, and take their chance on probation at the magistrates court. The attempted break-in had the appearance of a minor nuisance rather than a major crime. If Fairfax could manage to hold both youths until the next officer arrived, the entire incident would be over and done with in a few minutes. The posse would return to the station and Fairfax could get ahead with his paperwork.

PC Norman Harrison had got on to a parallel roof of the warehouse and overlooked the flat roof, except that the darkness made it difficult to see much. So far, he had picked out Fairfax but neither Craig nor Bentley. Then he called out, asking Fairfax if he was all right.

'I've got one,' Fairfax called back, 'There's another one on the roof.'

At that moment, Harrison saw Bentley with Fairfax holding on to him.

In almost total darkness, Fairfax who kept hold of Bentley – with Craig in front of them – edged round the sides of the brick stack as if in some ritual formation. The three of them moved round two sides of the stack and came on to the open roof again. It was now, according to Fairfax, that Bentley broke away from him. Bentley denied it. According to three police witnesses, though Bentley denied this as well, he shouted, 'Let him have it, Chris!'

In Fairfax's own words, 'There was then a flash and a loud report, and I felt something strike my right shoulder which caused me to spin round and fall to the ground.'

A good deal of the evidence was in conflict, if only because of the darkness and confusion on the roof. Fairfax recalled that he had been shot from a range of six feet. Craig insisted that it was thirty-seven feet. In that case he was lucky to hit Fairfax at all, since the sawing off of the gun-barrel made the Eley .455 accurate only to within six feet at such a distance.

As Fairfax picked himself up, he saw his two adversaries moving away to the right and left of him. Unarmed himself, he was still the only officer on the roof, facing two men. At least one of them had a gun. Perhaps they both did. The minor nuisance of the attempted break-in was suddenly a major police operation. Fairfax turned and shouted down from the roof, warning the men below that the intruders had guns. As yet he had no idea whether there might be more than two fugitives on the various roofs of the warehouse. If there were several, all of them armed, then his own situation might be perilous in the extreme.

At least it was simple enough for Fairfax to raise the alarm. According to civilian witnesses like Mrs Tennent who lived two doors away, it was easy to hear what was being said on the roof. Fairfax's message was passed on, the wireless car at the front of the building communicating the first news of the heightened emergency to Croydon police station. To reduce the odds against him, Fairfax grabbed at the nearer of the two men on the roof and knocked him to the ground with his fist. It was Bentley again. As Fairfax knocked him down, there was a second explosion. Craig fired again, but from further off.

Fairfax dragged Bentley to his feet, 'I pulled him up in front of me as a shield,' he explained. The immediate danger was that this prisoner might also have a gun. He forced Bentley behind one of the tall glass roof-lights and felt his clothing. 'He was not carrying a gun, but in his right-hand coat pocket was a knuckleduster.' Fairfax also found the sheath-knife in the breast-pocket of the coat.

'That's all I've got, guv'nor,' Bentley said reassuringly, 'I haven't got a gun.'

There was no longer any question of Fairfax being able to deal with Craig at the same time. His best hope was to get Bentley off the roof by going down through the doorway at the head of the stairs. As yet, that door was locked and barred from the inside.

'I'm going to work you round the roof to that escape door over there,' Fairfax said.

Bentley was apprehensive. 'He'll shoot you,' he said.

Fairfax drew his prisoner back in a semi-circle towards the well-head of the staircase. Craig followed them, unable to shoot without hitting Bentley rather than the policeman. At a few feet, he had scarcely been able to miss Fairfax. But the inaccuracy of the sawn-off revolver and the effect of the improvised ammunition made it impossible to aim with any certainty over the present distance. Once again, from the stack to the staircase door, the revolver would not have been accurate within six feet of the point aimed at. Craig started retreating towards the shelter of the brick stack where the struggle had begun.

Behind him, Fairfax heard one of his colleagues on the drainpipe. He shouted at Craig again.

'Drop your gun.'

'Come and get it!'

PC McDonald had followed Fairfax. Seeing a wet footprint on a window-sill by the drainpipe, he had chosen that way up. But McDonald was a weightier man and was having difficulty at the top of the pipe. He got to within six feet of the roof and heard a voice shout, 'Let him have it, Chris.' Unlike Fairfax, he did not recall that this was followed by a shot. McDonald, stuck on the pipe, began to climb down again. Then he heard the first shots fired and made a second attempt to get to Fairfax. By now, Fairfax had got Bentley back at the edge of the roof by the drainpipes. It was also behind the shelter of the staircase well-head. From there, he was able to help McDonald up the last part of his second climb. That he was able to do so suggests that Bentley had given up the struggle and showed no further inclination to escape. He sat on the low brick wall at the edge of the roof and made no attempt to get away while Fairfax assisted McDonald. He was soon held on either side by the two policemen.

McDonald, who could make out Craig in the darkness at the far end of the roof, was told by Fairfax, 'He got me in the shoulder.'

'I told the silly bugger not to use it,' Bentley was alleged to have said in response to this. He kept up a commentary on the conversation between the two policemen, as if he was now trying to distance himself from Craig's actions. Though his remarks showed that he knew Craig owned a gun, as most of his schoolfriends had known it, there was nothing that specifically proved Bentley's knowledge that Craig was carrying the gun that night. 'I told the silly bugger not to use it,' given Bentley's vagueness and feebleness of expression, might equally mean, 'I knew he'd brought it but I told him not to use it,' or 'I knew he owned it but I told him not to bring it.'

While all this was going on at one side of the building, PC Norman Harrison had moved forward from the parallel roof of the warehouse, where it was joined to the rear of the flat roof by a surface of sloping asbestos tiles. But though Harrison might have taken Craig from the other side, the approach along a sloping roof was difficult. Indeed, it soon became perilous. Craig saw the light of the policeman's torch and fired a shot in his direction. Harrison dropped the torch, which rolled down into the gutter at the edge of the roof. Then he took cover against a chimney stack, only to hear a second shot and the impact of a bullet hitting the brickwork that sheltered him.

Like the other officers, Harrison was still unarmed. There was nothing for him to do but withdraw cautiously the way he had come. Fairfax and McDonald could see what was happening but could do nothing to help. As Harrison climbed down, the two policemen were marooned on the roof with one prisoner and a gunman. They had no means of opening the locked door in the well-head of the staircase, which was in any case in Craig's field of fire. To get down the drain-pipe, with or without Bentley, was out of the question. They could only take cover behind the wall of the staircase access and wait.

As Craig fired at Harrison, McDonald asked, 'What sort of a gun has he got, Fairy?'

Again, it was Bentley who was alleged to have answered, as if anxious to be of help.

'He's got a .45 Colt and plenty of bloody ammunition too.'

In court this was once again taken as proof that Bentley knew Craig was carrying the gun that night, rather than that he knew the gun Craig possessed was a '.45 Colt'. Craig liked to boast of it under this name, though it was a gun of a different sort.

Tamworth Road had become a scene of much activity and a good deal of confusion. Two ambulances had arrived with bells ringing and there was the clang of a fire-engine bell as its officers arrived and began to put up an extension ladder to the roof. The residents of the surrounding houses had been brought to their doors by the sound of the shots. In the Robert Peel public house, the landlord and his customers had heard them. The last house at the cinema ended early on Sunday evening and it seems that the audience at one performance had exchanged film drama for the real thing. Not least among the difficulties of the police was holding the crowds back and out of danger.

The first alarm had also gone out to Scotland Yard and to neighbouring police forces. Recalling memories of the siege of Sidney Street in 1910, with riflemen of the Scots Guards shooting it out with Anarchists in the East End, police commanders were taking no chances. No one knew yet how many gunmen there might be on this roof and the other roofs surrounding it. Nor was it known who they were or what they intended to do.

Guns had been issued at Croydon police station, as the immediate danger to Fairfax and his colleagues became clear. Inspector Bodley was on the scene and Detective Chief Inspector John Leslie Smith was on his way. Reinforcements of armed police had been despatched from other divisions and uniformed police were brought in to control the crowds. There were police on the drainpipes and on the roofs of neighbouring buildings. The warehouse was surrounded and the only question was whether the sixteen-year-old gunman would come down from the roof dead or alive. His last chance of escape had long since been lost.

How to take him was another matter. The police on the spot might have sat tight and waited for the guns to arrive. But while they did that, the lives of Fairfax and McDonald – and Bentley himself – remained in danger. Harrison reached the ground and described what he had seen. At the same time, Sidney Miles had arrived with the key-holder and the keys to the main door of the warehouse. The building was unlocked. Leading the way, with

Harrison behind him, Miles made for the staircase that led up to the roof. The guns had still not arrived from Croydon police station but now, at least, the second group of officers had no need to shin up drainpipes or edge their way along a sloping roof in sight of the gunman.

At the top of the stairs, the door was fastened by a bar. Miles pushed the bar up with some difficulty and then kicked the door open. Fairfax shouted out, telling the staircase group that he and McDonald, with their prisoner, were to one side of the well-head. Miles sprang out on to the roof to join them and there was a shot. Harrison saw Miles fall back with blood over his face. It was evident at once that he was mortally injured. He fell dead, the bullet entering his forehead just above the left eyebrow and exiting at the back of his head. A second shot rang out, apparently hitting the door-frame of the staircase well-head. Harrison could see the figure of the gunman, holding his revolver with both hands. No one among the policemen on the staircase yet had a firearm. Harrison was now in the doorway of the well-head and found himself leading the attack, still unarmed. In desperation, he threw his truncheon at Craig, followed by a block of wood and a bottle of milk that he had picked up as a weapon.

The missiles fell without effect on the asphalt roof and the adversary identified himself at last.

'I am Craig,' he shouted, 'You've just given my brother twelve years. Come on, you coppers. I'm only sixteen.'

CHAPTER 5

As Sidney Miles fell dead at the feet of his colleagues, the scene on the warehouse roof remained one of darkness and confusion. Fairfax and McDonald, with Bentley in their custody, were still sheltering behind the staircase well-head. When Miles fell, McDonald was nearest to him. He saw the terrible injury to the victim's face, pulled him behind the shelter of the well-head brickwork and knew at once that Miles was dead. Bentley, standing by, could only grasp that Miles had been badly hurt. Harrison could still see Craig, who had come out from behind the stack and was holding his gun in both hands. Jumping forward from the doorway, Harrison then joined Fairfax and the others on the roof. As he did so, Craig fired another shot at him and missed, hitting the open doorway of the stairway. PC Robert Jaggs, the last man to attempt a climb by way of the drainpipe, had just come over the parapet.

There were now four policemen alive and one dead behind the well-head wall, in addition to Bentley. Jaggs put his head round the corner of the brickwork to see where Craig was. Each time that he tried to look, another shot echoed across the roof. Then he heard a shout from Craig.

'Come on you brave coppers! Think of your wives!'

Jaggs drew back and Bentley said anxiously, 'You want to look out. He'll blow your heads off.'

Fairfax and Harrison then decided to try and get Bentley out of the way. They would take him round the well-head's open door, down the stairway, and hand him over. As they began this manoeuvre, Bentley shouted, 'They're taking me down, Chris!'

Craig seemed to be firing at anything that moved on the roof. As Bentley later said in evidence, it was not just a matter of protecting his own skin, 'He might have shot anybody.' When the two policemen and their prisoner were already on the stairs, Craig called out, 'Have they hurt you, Derek?'

There was no reply. Craig fired again in the direction of the well-head.

Fairfax and Harrison got Bentley down to the foot of the stairs and handed him over. It was about twenty minutes since Fairfax and the first uniformed men had reached Tamworth Road. In response to the general alarm, a collection of police firearms had now arrived in a despatch bag. According to Fairfax's recollection in 1975, the bag was handed to Inspector Cook in the Managing Director's office of the warehouse, at the point when Bentley had just been taken down the stairs. If this were so, it would make nonsense of any theory that Miles was shot in error by a police marksman from somewhere on another roof. No guns would have been available to the police at the time that Miles was killed. The suggestion that the opening of the door might have been taken by such a hypothetical marksman as Bentley breaking away from custody does not stand up to examination in any case. Bentley was on the roof. The police had not so far been able to open the door. Whoever else might be coming out, it could certainly not have been Bentley.

At ground level, there was activity and confusion. Mrs Tennent, who lived two doors away from the warehouse, told reporters an hour or two later, 'We were watching the television when we first heard the sound of firing. We thought at first it was fireworks.' Guy Fawkes night was on the next Wednesday and several of those who first heard the shots assumed that someone was letting off squibs and bangers.

'Then a neighbour shouted that shooting was taking place and everyone rushed to the front door,' Mrs Tennent added, 'Within a matter of minutes dozens of police had arrived. One of the first things they did was to tell people to keep off the street and under cover. Some police came through our house and went into the back garden, which adjoins that of the shop. From inside, we could hear intermittent shooting and a man shouting at the top of his voice. I heard him say, "Come on. I am enjoying myself!"'

This, at least, suggests that the voices on the roof could be clearly heard over some distance and even in the neighbouring houses. At the same time the fire-brigade, which had already put up an extension ladder, began to run out hoses. It was unlikely that they were about to turn them on the gunman. With the siege of Sidney Street in mind, it was a precaution against the cornered criminals setting fire to the building.

By now, the landlord and customers of the Robert Peel public house had heard the shots outside and swelled the crowd in the road. Henry Hickman, whose home adjoined the warehouse on the other side to Mrs Tennent, confirmed that armed police were now being deployed. 'Police with guns in their hands walked through my house to get to the back of the building. They warned us to get out of the way. I could see two men squatting on the roof. Only one of them was firing.' One of the crowd added, 'I could see two men on the roof in the flash of police torches. One looked quite young.'

Such was the scene about twenty minutes after the incident had begun. The eyewitness accounts confirm that there was still a good deal of confusion as to who was who and what was going on. Fairfax, who had brought Bentley down to ground level, was in the best position to know. He was duly issued with a .32 revolver and went back up the stairs, the first armed officer to reach the roof.

From within the staircase well-head, he shouted at Craig, 'Drop your gun! I also have a gun!'

Back came the scornful reply from the darkness.

'Come on then, copper! Let's have it out! Are you hiding behind a shield? Is it bullet-proof? Are we going to have a shooting-match? It's just what I like!'

Some weeks later, Craig was asked what he thought his situation was as he stood there on the roof, gun in hand, offering to take on all comers.

'In a film or something,' he said.

It was just what the critics of cinema sex-and-violence wanted to hear. To Craig it was also a convenient moral alibi. And, in truth, Tamworth Road had taken on the look of a film location. In less than half an hour, the drab Sunday night quiet of commercial Croydon had embraced the plot of a last-reel encounter as acted out by Bogart or Cagney. Fairfax jumped from the well-head on to the roof. When he did so there was another flash from Craig's gun in the darkness and a loud report. But police training gave Fairfax an advantage over his inexperienced adversary.

Instead of meeting the gunman head-on, Fairfax ran in a semi-circle, firing twice at Craig as he did so to keep his enemy's head down. In the darkness and uncertainty, it would then be a matter of shooting to kill. Warning shots were the stuff of fiction. A bullet fired into the ground might ricochet almost anywhere. To fire into the air would endanger policemen now climbing out on to the surrounding roofs. Fairfax could not be expected to know their locations but he must have been well aware that they were there. By the same token, he was on his own. No other officer was likely to risk firing at Craig on the flat roof with Fairfax moving upon it, unable to get a clear view of his identity or position.

As Fairfax ran in a semi-circle, PC Stewart was in Burr's engineering yard adjoining the rear corner of the warehouse. Looking up, he could see the right-angle edge of the roof that ran round two sides between the brick stack and the well-head of the stairs. Craig was sitting on the guard-rail at that corner of the roof with his feet out in front of him, holding his gun in both hands, aiming it at Fairfax and firing.

After the last shot at Fairfax, Stewart heard him fire again. This time there was only a click. Four times Craig tried to fire and each time there was nothing but the dry click of the revolver as the chambers turned. Then he pointed the revolver in the air. Now, when he pulled the trigger, it fired for the last time.

'See?' said Craig, 'It's empty.'

In the romantic-heroic film tradition of the cornered gunman, he swung his legs over the guard-rail of the roof and stood on the parapet.

'Well, here we go,' he said, adding, 'Give my love to Pam.'

The policeman on the roof failed to catch the girl's name. Head-first, as if taking the plunge into a swimming-bath, Craig dived from the warehouse roof. There was a wooden-framed glass-house at the rear of the engineering yard, about ten feet from the corner of the warehouse. Stewart saw Craig falling through the darkness. His body hit the wooden frame of the glass-house roof and fell from there to the ground. It was his gun that broke one of the panes.

Stewart, taking no chances, ran across and jumped on the fugitive. Craig was still conscious.

'I wish I was fucking dead,' he said, 'I hope I've killed the fucking lot.'

It was the first of such remarks attributed to him in the days that followed, creating the legend of the embittered teenage gunman who had killed without remorse. When asked at his trial if he expressed sorrow or even regret for the death of Sidney Miles to anyone at the time, Craig was unable to think of such a person.

Craig was not dead nor likely to die. A fall of twenty-two feet, broken seven or eight feet above the ground by the frame of the glass-house roof was not enough for that. But he had fractured his spine, his breast-bone and his left wrist. While Bentley was bundled into the back of a police car with a sergeant and a constable either side of him, one of the ambulances was brought round to Drayton Place, at the rear of the warehouse, to take Craig to Croydon General Hospital. It was then just after ten o'clock. Little more than an hour before, Bentley had been watching television in his parents' sitting room. Craig had been on the street-corner in Norwood with his friends. Sidney Miles had set out for what promised to be a quiet shift. Now, as the gun battle ended, the other ambulance prepared to take the dead policeman to Croydon's Mayday Mortuary. PC Norman Harrison, who had himself narrowly escaped two of Craig's bullets a little while before, was detailed to escort the body of his colleague there.

With improbable and chilling rapidity, such apparently mundane destinies had fused in a crime that was to dominate English public life as no other had done since Sidney Street or Crippen more than forty years earlier.

Detective-Constable Fairfax was also taken to Croydon

General Hospital, where he was found to be in a state of shock. The bullet had grazed his shoulder but broken no bones. Craig lay on a couch in the next cubicle, where Detective-Sergeant Shepherd saw him less than an hour after his fall.

'How do you feel?' Shepherd asked.

'It's my back. It hurts.'

It went on hurting until just after two o'clock in the morning, when he was given codeine to dull the pain.

Detective-Sergeant Shepherd had been detailed to keep a watch on Craig at Croydon Hospital. Presently his prisoner said, 'I had six in the gun. I fired at a policeman. I had six tommy-gun bullets.'

Shepherd reminded him that anything he said might be used in evidence. Craig seemed not to care.

'Is the copper dead?' he asked, 'How about the others? We ought to have shot them all.'

When Shepherd had been there about half an hour, he was joined by the senior officer in the case, Detective Chief Inspector John Smith. Smith had arrived at Tamworth Road when the shooting was over. He left there after a little while and went to Mayday Mortuary to make a formal examination of Sidney Miles' body so that the investigation could proceed. The official identification was left to the policeman's widow, who had seen her husband off on his routine watch and had as yet no idea that he was dead.

'I am a police officer,' Smith said to Craig, 'I have just seen the dead body of Police Constable Miles in Mayday Mortuary, and as a result of inquiries I have made I charge you with his murder, together with Derek William Bentley.'

If Smith expected tears of contrition from the sixteen-year-old, he was disappointed.

'He's dead, is he?' Craig said, 'What about the others?'

There was to be no confession and no contrition. Smith, who was clearly wasting time by remaining, said, 'You will be detained here until you are fit to be moved.' With that he left.

Craig's account of the hour after the roof-top gun-battle was quite different. He swore that he remembered nothing from the time he dived off the roof until he woke up in hospital. There was no recollection of hitting the glass-house roof or lying in the yard below. He had not said the things attributed to him then or in Croydon Hospital.

'I was in hospital, and I woke up when someone hit me in the mouth and called me a murdering bastard,' he insisted, 'They were pushing me down a corridor on a trolley and they were running me into the walls and all over the bumps so they could hurt me.'

In support of Craig's account, it has to be said that Fairfax as reported by David Yallop almost twenty years later, recalled that he had shared the same ambulance with Craig. Craig had been unconscious and remained so until the following day. To accept that report, it is also necessary to accept that evidence given under oath by three other officers cannot be true.

Fairfax was still on the roof and out of earshot when Craig lay in the engineering yard and made the remarks reported by PC Stewart. If Craig lost consciousness after this, it would be consistent with Fairfax's memory of him being unconscious in the ambulance. At the hospital, according to the trial evidence, Fairfax was suffering from 'a certain degree of shock,' while being examined and treated by Dr Nicholas Jazwon, the casualty officer. It was also necessary for him to be x-rayed. Not until after 1am did he make a statement to his colleagues.

The sequence of events would hardly allow for Fairfax to keep a constant watch on Craig in the next cubicle to see whether he was conscious at some point, unconscious all the time, or conscious but in pain between 11 and 11.30pm. The hospital records show that at 2.15am Craig was given codeine to ease the pain. This would not have been done if he was unconscious. James Ross was the constable on duty when the codeine was given. He heard Craig say, 'Did I really kill a policeman?' And then a little later, 'I got the gun from a house in Purley. There are plenty more where that came from.'

If Craig's story of an unseen person running amok with the hospital trolley were true, the most likely time would have been when he was brought into the building. That it happened when he was taken to be x-rayed or to the operating theatre, late next morning, requires a belief that the hospital staff treated him in this way, that their colleagues turned a blind eye, and that Craig was unconscious until then. If it happened when he was brought into the building, if he was indeed unconscious and came round at that point, then he was presumably conscious soon afterwards when Detective-Sergeant Shepherd arrived. He was certainly conscious when he gave the name of Norman Parsley as his companion in the robbery of the South Croydon greengrocer, for the police raided Parsley's home that night, within hours of the shooting in Tamworth Road.

While Craig lay on the couch in his hospital cubicle, Bentley was in a cell at Croydon police station, where he had been brought at about the time of Craig's journey in the ambulance. When Sergeant Edward Roberts had arrived at the warehouse in Tamworth Road, Bentley had still not been brought down the stairs. After the shooting was over, Inspector Bodley handed over the prisoner to Roberts at the front of the building to be taken by car to Croydon police station. Roberts cautioned him and Bentley said, 'I didn't have a gun. Chris shot him.'

Bentley was bundled into the back of the car between Roberts and PC Alderson, with PC Henry Stephens driving. During the short journey to the police station, Bentley claimed that he was asked the name of the gunman and gave it as Christopher Craig. He was also asked what sort of gun Craig had and replied that he didn't know. Both Roberts and Stephens denied in evidence that these questions had been put. Their version of events was that Bentley said nothing until the car was approaching the George Street traffic lights at the centre of Croydon. Then he spoke, unprompted, 'I knew he had a gun, but I didn't think he'd use it. He's done one of your blokes in.'

Then, according to Stephens, Sergeant Roberts said, 'I should not make any other statement now. You will be given a chance to make a statement at the station.'

Bentley later denied making the remark, insisting that he did not know Craig was carrying a gun that night. Once again, assuming that he had spoken the words, they were taken to mean that he knew Craig had brought the gun with him that night. Given Bentley's fumbling with the English language, they might equally well have meant that he knew Craig owned a gun but didn't think he would use it for that evening's expedition. By denying the words altogether, he put himself in conflict with two more police witnesses. His evidence that he was asked while in the car what sort of gun Craig had and said he didn't know, also conflicted with the testimony of the police witnesses on the warehouse roof who swore that they heard him say, 'He's got a .45 Colt and plenty of bloody ammunition too.' The trial jury would have to take sides. Would they believe five policemen or a youth who admitted he was out to rob?

Sergeant Roberts' evidence in general is discounted by David Yallop on the grounds that it was contradicted by six other people. Roberts is said to have sworn in court that Bentley was brought down the warehouse stairs 'after the shooting was over.' That would certainly have contradicted six other witnesses, but Roberts did not say it. The record of the trial makes this plain. His evidence was that Bentley was first brought down the stairs. Later on, 'after the shooting was over', Bentley was handed over to him by Inspector Bodley at the front of the building. There was no contradiction in this at all. It is not, therefore, 'incredible' that Roberts should have followed procedure by cautioning Bentley 'with bullets still flying on the roof.' There were no bullets flying by that time.

At the police station, Bentley was searched and then locked in a cell, while the officers of Z Division waited for Detective Chief Inspector John Smith. He was then still visiting the warehouse roof, before going to the mortuary to examine the body of the dead policeman. Just after 11pm, Mrs Miles was informed that her husband had been killed on duty. By 11.30, Smith was at Croydon General Hospital.

The next procedure in the night's investigation was to search the homes of the Craig and Bentley families. At 1.15am, a police car with Sergeant Shepherd and two other officers drew up in Norbury Court Road. In a few moments more, the Craig family were roused and the house was searched. Under the floorboards of the attic, the sawn-off piece of the Eley .455 barrel was found, as well as a tin box of ammunition. A round of .45 ammunition lay under the pillow of Christopher Craig's bed.

Quarter of an hour later, the knocking of a second search-party woke the Bentley family a few streets away. Mr Bentley knew only that his son had gone out with Norman Parsley, variously described by Derek Bentley as 'a good bloke' and 'an educated bloke.' By midnight there was still no sign of Derek. The other members of the family went to bed, leaving his sister Iris to wait for him downstairs. When the knock at the door came, she prudently asked who was there.

'Police officers! ... Open that door! We're police officers!'

By the time that Mr Bentley got downstairs, the police were in the sitting room. To his questions, he received one answer.

'Your son has killed a man.'

A search of the house began at once. Uncle Albert was still asleep in the room he shared with Derek Bentley, when the police came in. To his reasonable demand as to what was going on, he too got one answer.

'You'll find out!'

Bentley's bedroom with its toys and clothes, its morse-code set bought for him last Christmas had an incongruity that was characteristic of him, though unlikely to be appreciated by the police officers who rummaged through its contents. Above his bed was a pin-up in the tight-blouse-and-briefs costume of the day. Above the pin-up, a framed text hung on the wall. *Casting all your care upon Him, for He careth for you.*

The search produced only a sheath-knife that Bentley had used in house-clearances, while working for the furniture-remover. To the further inquiries of the family, the police continued to say that Bentley had killed a man and that he was being held at Croydon police station. His father and uncle set off at once for Croydon. When they got there, Mr Bentley asked to see his son. The duty sergeant told him it was impossible. The sergeant refused to tell him more than that, except to say that a policeman had been shot. When asked if Bentley was accused of it, the duty sergeant replied, 'That's all I've got to say,' and walked off. He talked, said

Bentley's father later, 'indifferently, as if he hated the sight of me.'

With the searches over and Craig under sedation in his hospital cubicle, the focus of the inquiry was on Bentley. Much was said later of the intellectual feebleness obvious in the answers and statements of an illiterate and mentally subnormal youth. Added to this was the hour of night when the questioning took place. Few suspects, however mentally agile, would have seemed at their best by 4am.

Bentley seems to have had not the least idea of the peril in which he stood. He had been in Fairfax's custody for about quarter of an hour when Craig shot Sidney Miles. It was true that the two youths had set out as equal partners in crime to rob the warehouse. But Bentley insisted that he did not know Craig was carrying a gun. He also denied saying, 'Let him have it, Chris,' when Fairfax grabbed him, and he denied breaking away from the policeman's grip. Only when Craig's bullet hit Fairfax in the shoulder was that grip broken. And even then, Bentley said, he had not attempted to get away.

Bentley's intellectual grasp of such arguments was slight enough. But abler minds than his would have been astonished to suppose that, with the undisputed facts as they were and with Craig's life in no danger because of his age, Bentley stood already in the shadow of the gallows.

At 4am that Monday morning, after a visit from Superintendent Greene of Scotland Yard, Bentley was brought from his cell to Chief Inspector John Smith's office at Croydon police station. Detective-Sergeant Shepherd was also present. When Bentley was brought in, he looked at Smith and asked, 'Are you in charge of this case, guv'nor?'

'Yes,' said Smith.

'I didn't kill him, guv,' Bentley said, 'Chris did it.'

Smith cautioned him and Bentley said, perhaps hoping to convince his interrogators of his innocence, 'Let me tell you about it.'

'Very well, if you wish,' Smith said.

In the hour that followed, Bentley made his statement. At his trial, it was suggested that such a composition was quite beyond him. Certainly, he was incapable of writing it down. This was done for him by Detective-Sergeant Shepherd and signed by Bentley at the end as being correct. He was, of course, unable to read for himself what Shepherd had written.

The suggestion by the defence was that Bentley did not volunteer a statement in the required manner. The two policemen composed it by asking him questions and constructing a statement from his answers. Bentley's limited self-expression made it unlikely that the account could have been obtained in any other way. Both Detective-Sergeant Shepherd and Chief Inspector Smith denied this. On the other hand, they did not deny the difficulty in getting a statement from Bentley, who could only dictate small sections at a time. He asked repeatedly, 'What have I said before?'

The earlier part of the statement would then be read back to him.

Bentley's father might not be an impartial commentator on the manner in which the statement was taken. However, he made the reasonable point that it would have been beyond his son's ability to write it or even to dictate it, 'in the form in which it was written down.' Bentley, in his father's experience, would not even have known the meaning of some of the words used. But when Mr Bentley added that a phrase like, 'I should have mentioned,' was beyond his son's powers of utterance, he seemed to take his argument beyond the limit of credibility.

Bentley was later to insist that he was asked questions by Shepherd and Smith and that his answers were written down as if part of his statement. He also claimed that the statement contained answers he had not given. He had signed the document as true, none the less, because he could not read what it contained. The disadvantage of being a dim-witted teenager confronted by two detectives was bad enough. Much worse was to come when Bentley found himself fighting for his life against skilled cross-examination by Senior Treasury Counsel and the hostile interventions from the Lord Chief Justice.

The statement that he made, just before dawn in Chief Inspector Smith's room, was not a long one. However it was prompted, the short-lived mental impulses and flat-toned phrases, the disjointed thoughts and uncertain recollection, sound like the authentic voice of Derek Bentley.

I have known Craig since I went to school. We were stopped by our parents going out together, but we still continued going out with each other – I mean we have not gone out together until to-night.

I was watching television to-night (2nd November 1952) and between 8pm and 9pm Craig called for me. My mother answered the door and I heard her say that I was out. I had been out earlier to the pictures and got home just after 7pm.

A little later Norman Parsley and Frank Fazey called. I did not answer the door or speak to them. My mother told me that they had called and I then ran out after them. I walked up the road and with them to the paper shop where I saw Craig standing. We all talked together and then Norman Parsley and Frank Fazey left. Chris Craig and I then caught a bus to Croydon. We got off at West Croydon and then we walked down the road where the toilets are – I think it is Tamworth Road. When we came to the place where you found me, Chris looked in the window. There was a little iron gate at the side. Chris then jumped over and I followed. Up to then Chris had not said anything. We both got out on to the flat roof at the top. Then someone in a corner on the opposite side shone a torch up towards us. Chris said, 'It's a copper. Hide behind here.' We hid behind a shelter arrangement on the roof. We were there waiting for about ten minutes. I did not know he was going to use the gun.

A plain clothes man climbed up the drainpipe and on to the roof. The man said, 'I am a police officer. The place is surrounded.' He caught hold of me and as we walked away Chris fired. There was nobody else there at the time. The policeman and I then went round a corner by a door.

A little later the door opened and a policeman in uniform came out. Chris fired again then and this policeman fell down. I could see that he was hurt as a lot of blood came from his forehead just above his nose. The policemen dragged him round the corner behind the brickwork entrance to the door. I remember I shouted something but I forget what it was. I could not see Chris when I shouted to him. He was behind a wall. I heard some more policemen behind the door and the policeman with me said, 'I do not think he has many more bullets left.' Chris shouted, 'Oh yes, I have,' and fired again. I think I heard him fire three times altogether. The policeman then pushed me down the stairs and I did not see any more.

I knew we were going to break into the place. I did not know what we were going to get – just anything that was going. I did not have a gun and I did not know Chris had one until he shot. I now know that the policeman in uniform that was shot is dead.

I should have mentioned that after the plain clothes policeman got up the drainpipe and arrested me, another policeman in uniform followed and I heard someone call him Mac. He was with us when the other policeman was moved.

The limp style and jumbled order of events in the statement scarcely suggested that the police had done more than take down Bentley's words, whether volunteered or given in answer to questions. The ability to reconstruct systematically the drama on the warehouse roof was beyond Bentley's capacity. He recalled fragments of the encounter and could not even remember what it was he had shouted at Craig when Miles was killed. Craig was to recall that he himself had shouted out, 'Is he dead?' after he saw Miles fall, and that Bentley shouted back, 'Yes, he is, you rotten sod!' But this, like Bentley shouting, 'You bloody fool!' when Fairfax was hit in the shoulder, came too late to save his life.

Bentley broke down several times while making the statement, confused and shocked. A more callous or a more astute culprit would surely have added a claim as to the words he had shouted at Craig, even if he did so only as a desperate fabrication. Whatever they were, the dismay and confusion had wiped them from Bentley's uncertain memory.

He was presented with the statement to sign as correct, after it had been read over to him. Bentley tried. He misspelt his name 'Derek' as 'Derk.' He was asked to sign again and did so, after inquiring from the two policemen how to spell his own name. He later denied having said in the statement that he knew the break-in was to take place. Unable to read what he was signing, he had not known that the sentence was included.

At 5.30am, Chief Inspector Smith told him that he would be charged with being 'concerned' in the murder of PC Sidney Miles.

'Craig shot him,' Bentley repeated, 'I hadn't got a gun. He was with me on the roof and then shot him between the eyes.'

He was charged with the murder and cautioned again. This time Bentley said nothing. It was plain that he could not even begin to comprehend how he might be held responsible for a murder committed by another person, fifteen minutes or more after he had been arrested.

The press, the law, the government, and the Lord Chief Justice himself were about to enlighten Derek Bentley in that matter.

CHAPTER 6

Before Bentley or Craig had been interrogated, let alone charged, Fleet Street's later editions went to press with the most sensational murder story of mid-century. Even the officers of Z Division, Metropolitan Police, were not yet clear as to the precise sequence of events in the darkness and confusion during which the gun-shots had been exchanged. It was not until daylight that a proper search of the warehouse roof and the surrounding area could be carried out. The press would be bound to get the story wrong in its details. In the current state of public opinion, the tone of the reporting counted for more than the facts.

There was so much doubt as to what was going on that by no means all the papers gave the story banner headlines or front-page coverage. Some, like the *News Chronicle*, largely ignored it in favour of the impending victory of Dwight D Eisenhower in the next day's United States presidential election. Elsewhere, it contended for space against the more graphic violence of the Mau-Mau uprising against the British in Kenya, where a state of emergency had been declared. It was possible, depending on one's customary choice of newspaper, to know little or nothing about the case. Indeed, when Craig's counsel was phoned by his clerk two weeks later with news that he had been briefed, his immediate reply was, 'Craig – who's Craig?'

A vivid answer to that question had been given elsewhere within a few hours of the crime.

The more sedate reporting of the Croydon incident was that of the *Daily Telegraph's* LONDON PC SHOT DEAD FROM ROOF – DETECTIVE WOUNDED ON FIRE-ESCAPE – TWO MEN ARRESTED or even the *Daily Mirror's* PC SHOT DEAD, CID MAN HIT IN ROOF SIEGE, which headed the papers' front pages. But only one other story in 1952, the sudden death of King George VI on 6 February, could have rivalled this for shock headlines. Several of the Fleet Street papers made the most of it from the start on that Monday morning. The *Daily Mail* raised the temperature of its readers with a headlined report that owed more to newsroom fantasy than to the trade of reporting: CHICAGO GUN BATTLE IN LONDON – GANGSTERS WITH MACHINE-GUN ON ROOF KILL DETECTIVE, WOUND ANOTHER. The writer made the first of innumerable comparisons with the siege of Sidney Street, describing hand-to-hand fighting and armed police shooting back. When the police first arrived in Tamworth Road, a siege of that kind seemed to them at least a possibility. They might have faced several gunmen and an arsenal of weapons. In less than half an hour the shooting was over. Long before the press reports were written, it was evident that there had never been the least likelihood of anything on that scale.

Some of the mistakes were explicable if not excusable. Apart from smaller calibre bullets, Craig had used in his revolver .45 ammunition designed for automatic weapons. These rounds were referred to at his trial as 'tommy-gun bullets,' a description he had used himself while in hospital. In some reports of the shooting, the press chose to assume that this ammunition had been fired from the usual weapon. Craig and Bentley were duly described as machine-gunning police over the Croydon rooftops. Armed officers had converged on Tamworth Street from Scotland Yard and the Metropolitan area in a shoot-out that would have put Bogart, Cagney and Raft to shame.

The murdered policeman was sometimes referred to as a 'detective' and sometimes correctly as a uniformed officer, married with two children, who had served for twenty years in the force. However uncertain and inaccurate these first reports might be, the message from Fleet Street to the breakfast tables and commuter trains of England was clear. The shadow of Al Capone and Lucky Luciano had fallen across suburban Croydon during the previous night. Where would it fall next? No one could feel safe, least of all the police who were in the front line of this shooting war.

The press was debarred from overt comment on the case until there had been a trial and a verdict. But in the next few days there was implicit comment in abundance. On 4 November, the *Daily Herald* was one of the papers to take up the issue of firearms – legal and illegal – in its front-page story, WHO HAS GUNS FOR SALE? NEW POLICE PROBE. By Thursday, two days later, the focus was on the 'menace of the thug,' the plight of 'old folk afraid to go to bed,' or the *Daily Telegraph's* choice of 'women going in fear.'

Even on that first morning of Monday 3 November 1952, when the attention of the press and its readers was directed upon Croydon, there was a sense in the reports that this was a decisive moment for the whole nation. It was now or never, in the country's determination to stop the rot.

More mundanely, at the scene of the crime in the cordoned-off area of Tamworth Road, a police seach-party was meticulously scrutinising the roof of the Barlow and Parker warehouse, as well as the surrounding gardens and yards, for spent bullets, cartridge cases, and any other evidence of the previous night's battle. Craig's revolver had been found easily at the time, having smashed through a pane in the glass-house roof as he fell.

By 11am, PC Bernard Beard from Croydon, a mild-mannered police draughtsman, was taking measurements of the warehouse and surrounding buildings, from which he would produce a plan to scale. He was accompanied by Chief Inspector Percy Law from Scotland Yard's Photographic Department, who was taking pictures of the flat asphalt roof, the passage at the side of the building, and the glass-house on to which Craig had fallen.

Press interest soon turned to Croydon magistrates' court. Those who waited outside to see Bentley's arrival were disappointed. He was brought through a tunnel under the street, which connected the police cells with the court building. The benches in the court were crowded with reporters, though there was not much more to report about the gun battle itself. The *Star* got the story out first in page-wide headlines on the front of its Late Night edition. COURT STORY OF ROOF SHOOTING – PC MURDER CHARGE NAMES 2 YOUTHS. Craig did not, of course, appear in court but his name was revealed when Bentley's statement was read out. Bentley said little during the hearing, which was brief and formal. After the charge of murder was read out he replied simply, 'Not me, sir.'

Asked if he understood the charge, he said, 'Yes, I understand.'

Did he wish to put any questions to the police witness?

'No, sir.'

He was also asked if he wanted legal aid.

'I will see my father,' he said.

The statement was given with his reply, 'Craig did it.' And that was that. His first public appearance had lasted for just three minutes. The jostling and pushing began, the first flashbulbs popping, as he was led away and driven from the court to Brixton prison by police car. A barrage of cameras clicked and popped as the car edged out into the street between the pushing onlookers. Unlike most English murders, this one had the promise of being a story with international appeal – at least of interest in Europe and the Commonwealth. The Syndicated International photographer caught Bentley sitting in the back of the car between the stolid well-fleshed figures of Chief Inspector Smith and Detective-Sergeant Shepherd in their raincoats and trilby hats. Bentley's own coat collar was turned up and his face pressed down into it. The light caught his slickly oiled and waved fair hair. By that evening, the world saw him for what he was. Next morning, YOUTH, 19, CHARGED WITH KILLING A POLICEMAN and variations on the theme promised the public that justice was going to be done.

Hedging its bets, Fleet Street opened negotiations with the families of the two accused murderers. The *Sunday Pictorial* bought the Craigs' story for £350 and put them under the care of Harry Proctor, so that they should not be poached. The *Sunday Dispatch* was later to buy the rights to the Bentleys' story, while the *Sunday Pictorial* made an offer for any final letter that Bentley might write to his family from the condemned cell. But Bentley seemed the less newsworthy of the pair at first and there was little urgency in concluding a deal for his story. The Craigs were more interesting and, in the case of their daughter Lucy, more glamorous than the worn and proletarian Bentleys.

A short distance away from the court proceedings, on that first morning, Craig was given an anaesthetic at Croydon General Hospital for an operation to set his broken wrist. He was unconscious until later that afternoon.

Sir Harold Scott, Commissioner of Metropolitan Police since 1945, had arrived in Croydon from Scotland Yard to talk to the uniformed officers who had been on the warehouse roof – Fairfax was still in hospital. But they were 'less interested in the night's events than concerned for the widow of the shot policeman, Miles. My impression, indeed, was that I had gone into a family home where one of the family had suddenly died.' Later, the commissioner visited Fairfax, 'an educated, thoughtful type, more like a clerk than a policeman, and a fighting one at that.' He was struck by the modesty, clarity, and lack of egotism with which Fairfax gave his account.

There was a further reason for concern among Miles' colleagues, which Sir Harold tastefully ignored. A man who behaved with the courage and impetuosity of Sidney Miles, and who gave his life in the course of his duty, earned a pension for his widow and children. But the government, however grateful for his loyalty and sacrifice, saw no reason to keep the bereaved in luxury. Mrs Miles was awarded £2 16s a week, or £2.80 after decimalisation.

Among other travellers to Croydon that morning was Dr David Haler, the pathologist who was to perform a post-mortem on the body of Sidney Miles. The results of this were to be debated during and after the trial. But the policemen to whom Dr Haler spoke that day repeated the allegation that when Bentley was grabbed by Fairfax on the roof, he had said, 'Let him have it, Chris!' If this was so, it would make it difficult to sustain the suggestion that the police witnesses involved in the case concocted the words later in order to ensure Bentley's conviction for murder.

In a number of matters during the trial, it was to be suggested that police witnesses might have compared or edited their evidence. The allegations are now beyond proof or disproof but they suffer the disadvantage of interpreting attitudes in 1952 as if they belonged to the 1970s and 1980s. There were, no doubt, corrupt policemen in 1952 but there was also a sense in which because the police were expected to be honourable and truthful, they were. By 1977, the publication of such books as the Penguin Special, *The Fall of Scotland Yard*, revealed corruption in the Metropolitan Police on a scale that managed to be frightening and farcical at the same time. Ten years later, a programme on police brutality like Central Television's *Reasonable Force* in July 1987 is likely to horrify by its documented accounts of serious injuries inflicted deliberately by policemen on those who have committed no offence. Still more telling is the philosophy that a policeman successfully sued in a civil court for assault cannot automatically be subject to internal inquiry or discipline because a higher degree of proof may be needed. Cynicism inevitably breeds corruption. If the public no longer assume or expect that a police officer is honest, the police officer may be less likely to be so. That cynicism and its effects were far less common in 1952. Yet the mood of the police was certainly that the perpetrators of this crime should be shown no mercy.

As for the newspapers in the late autumn and mid-winter of 1952, the first shock of the press reports was to be followed by revelations of Craig's comments on the crime he had committed. He was under police guard in Croydon General Hospital when he came round from the anaesthetic later that Monday afternoon. PC John Smith was one of the men who had just come on watch when Craig woke up between 5pm and 6pm.

'You're coppers,' Craig said, seeing the men beside his bed, 'Ha! The other one's dead with a hole in his head!'

Then he pointed to himself.

'I'm all right. All you bastards should be dead.'

After that it seems that Craig went to sleep again. He woke once more at about 6.30pm and said to PC Vincent Denham, 'Is he dead?'

'Who?' Denham asked.

'That copper. I shot him in the head and he went down like a ton of bricks.'

Denham conceded that Craig was in great pain and not normal when he spoke these words. That did not prevent them from being reported and becoming public knowledge. Craig was given pethadrine at 9.45 on Monday evening to deaden the pain. Despite his condition, the vindictiveness of the words that followed did nothing to subdue the mood of public anger towards the two young criminals. There were those who felt it wrong to hang Bentley if Craig could escape by virtue of being under eighteen. Others began to think and say that the remedy was to lower the age for hanging so that both criminals could be executed.

Nor was this the last that Craig was reported as saying while in hospital. Two days later, during the afternoon, he said to PC Thomas Sheppard, 'Is the policeman I shot in the shoulder still in hospital? I know that the one I shot in the head is dead.'

Sheppard made no reply. Later that afternoon, Craig tried again.

'What do you get for carrying a knuckleduster? Bentley had mine.'

Still Sheppard was not drawn into conversation.

'Did you see the gun I had?' Craig asked, 'It was all on the wobble, so I took it to work and sawed two inches off the barrel.'

During the next afternoon, 6 November, PC Ernest Brown was on watch.

Craig said, 'If I hadn't cut a bit off the barrel of my gun, I would probably have killed a lot more policemen. That night I was out to kill because I had so much hate inside me for what they did to my brother. I shot the policeman in the head with my .45. If it had been the .22 he might not have died.'

Even if his remarks grew less vindictive during the week, he continued to show a lack of remorse, a callousness, an indifference to the grief and plight of Mrs Miles and her children that embittered those who read of such things.

In almost every respect, historical, geographical, and social, the murder of Sidney Miles brought two cultures into collision. To their elders, the diligent workers of the 1930s and the participants in the Finest Hour of World War Two, Bentley and Craig were nothing short of a moral aberration. Their conduct, like that of the criminal generation and class they represented, dishonoured the past and threatened the future. The sacrifices of the 1930s and the greater sacrifices of the war years had offered that generation a world free from want and ignorance. Health and housing, education and employment, had improved beyond recognition for the young and the poor in the post-war years. This was the thanks returned to the providers.

Adolescent violence of a kind was sought out as proof of manhood, a Saturday night substitute for the sport that was lauded as good for the middle-class character. There was nothing original in this, apart from a certain variation in costume and custom. To be a National Serviceman, for example, was to witness the contemporaries of Bentley and Craig in the uniforms of conscripts. They were a minority but they attracted the most public attention. The Saturday night fight with locals at dance-hall or dog-track was part of their masculine ritual in coming of age, even in such unlikely venues as the De La Warr Pavilion at Bexhill-on-Sea. Small wonder that parents looked askance at their daughters' enthusiasm for palais and jazz club. In January 1953, four Yorkshire headmasters were reported to 'deplore the effect of 'teen age dances on schoolgirls and are seeking to ban the girls from attending them.' This became the subject of solemn analysis and articles in the press by the sociologically qualified, a finely balanced warning and reassurance to worried mothers and fathers.

So far as ritual violence went, there lingered in that Saturday night stratum of teenage society something like the Zulu custom in which the right to possess a woman had to be earned by washing one's spear in the blood of an enemy. Her Majesty's services did not provide spears. A webbing-belt was the more usual weapon. Civilians like Craig and Bentley must equip themselves as they could.

This and much more was highlighted by the Croydon shooting and the case that followed. In the first two weeks of November 1952, though the press was muzzled in its opinions by the legal process, there were several events, routine and necessary, that demonstrated clearly the opinion of Croydon and the revulsion of the nation.

The inquest on PC Sidney Miles was held as soon as possible, three days after his death. To report it was to highlight at once the tragedy of his widow and two children, Mrs Miles having suffered the additional ordeal of identifying her husband's body. She was required to give evidence of this at the inquest. Within a few days, her married life had been replaced by a nightmare of grief and unwelcome publicity. The other witness, Dr Haler, had performed his post-mortem the day after Miles had been shot. His findings were straightforward enough. A large calibre bullet had entered the policeman's forehead above the left eyebrow – 'between the eyes,' as Bentley said – and left an exit wound at the rear of his head. There seemed no pretext for dispute or even debate in the matter. That being the case, there was no reason why the funeral should be delayed. Arrangements were made for Miles to be cremated and his ashes scattered in the first week of the case.

CORONER PRAISES FEARLESS POLICE, the *Daily Telegraph's* headline on Thursday morning, was typical of the Fleet Street reports. The police had been fearless and deserved the praise. Yet the sentiment that was gathering in the wake of the reports was an ill omen for the pair who must stand trial. For them there was worse to come, and it came the following morning. WAVE OF CRIME 'A CHALLENGE' – ARCHDEACON'S PLEA AT PC'S FUNERAL.

At the adjournment of the inquest, the body of the murdered policeman had been released for burial. It was on Thursday, four days after his death, that his funeral took place at Croydon Parish Church. He was buried with full police honours. The large congregation was led by the Home Secretary, Sir David Maxwell Fyfe, and the Commissioner of Metropolitan Police, Sir Harold Scott.

One man present at the funeral was to play a central role in the drama of Bentley's life and death. Sir David Maxwell Fyfe was a Scottish lawyer and a Conservative MP since 1935. He seemed to be diligent rather than exceptionally gifted. His was not a name that rang through the gladiatorial contests of pre-war murder trials. Indeed, it had not rung anywhere very much. During the war, he had at first been a military lawyer and became Deputy Chief Prosecutor at the Nuremberg War Crimes Tribunal. In appearance he was a well-fleshed man whose smooth bald head, in the circumstances of the day, had an unfortunate and unfair hint of Mussolini. But Maxwell Fyfe was no Mussolini. He was an unspectacular Tory, Solicitor-General in 1942 and briefly Attorney-General in 1945. With the return of a Conservative government in 1951, Churchill had made him Home Secretary. He was now just fifty-one but there was a sense in which the call to political greatness seemed to have come too faintly and far too late. He was not a man for the new world, let alone for the generation that Craig and Bentley represented. Though his virtues commended him to his own party, he was unlikely to appeal to the new voters in the electorate of the 1950s. That he did not do so was, in great part, a consequence of his behaviour in this case.

But Maxwell Fyfe was already in an unenviable situation. He was responsible for the police force. Most of all, he was responsible for showing it support and loyalty during such a time as that of Miles's death. But, in the end, it was also his responsibility to decide whether a man convicted of such a crime as the policeman's murder should be reprieved or go to the gallows. Whatever he did, Maxwell Fyfe would incur reproach from some quarter. It was a time during which legal considerations must be tempered by political sensitivity of the finest quality. This proved to be quite beyond him. He had about as much in common with Derek Bentley's patterns of thought and social conduct as he had with an Eskimo or a Bushman. Though he had been president of the Gordon Smith Institute for Seamen, he had lived in a self-confident world of Edinburgh and Oxford, Gray's Inn and the House of Commons, comfortably remote from life and death as it was known in Fairview Road, Norbury. In his conduct he was, without meaning to be, one of those who did most to bring closer the abolition of capital punishment.

The funeral of Sidney Miles was an expression of moral solidarity. Newspaper reports of the occasion centred on the address by the Venerable Charles Tonks, Archdeacon of Croydon.

His words confirmed the public's worst fears about the 'rising tide' of crime.

> The present wave of robbery with violence and armed resistance is foreign to this country. It is seriously disturbing the minds and the consciences of us all.
>
> Women are going in fear – fear of opening their doors after dark, fear of walking alone in quiet roads. Single-handed shopkeepers look askance at strange customers, and the thought may cross the minds of the police, will they find a gunman, where they might expect a petty thief?
>
> This is not England, the England we have known and for which men and women have laid down their lives.

The last sentence was one which would have attracted almost universal support and approval from those who read it. But the Archdeacon had not done. He went on to sound a familiar theme, that reforming the law and showing consideration to the criminal now outweighed 'due concern for the victims of the vicious, and for those who are in potential danger from the criminal and the desperate.'

Finally, he reminded his congregation and the invisible millions of newspaper readers of the remedy which the law had injudiciously abolished several years before.

> I would suggest even corporal punishment is not necessarily ruled out of consideration as a deterrent against vicious attacks.

There was a certain logic in this. If it could be shown that the flogging of Bentley and Craig for their first offences would have saved the life of Sidney Miles, it would have been impossible to argue against it. That it had not been shown was the weakness in the proposition. Even so, there seemed perhaps something odd about a legal system that found it abhorrent to birch an offender but entirely proper to put him to death.

The body of Sidney Miles was cremated and his ashes scattered in Croydon cemetery, where the mortal remains of Derek Bentley were to join his many years later. Perhaps it was appropriate that this final resting place was scarcely a mile to the north of the warehouse roof on which Miles had fallen and a little way south from the prison room where Bentley was to be hanged.

CHAPTER 7

The week following the Croydon 'gun battle' ended in something of an anti-climax. With the first and most sensational reports of the crime growing stale, the victim buried and the eulogies of 'fearless police' and the 'wave of crime' warnings over, there was little more that the press could do for the moment.

Bentley was on remand in Brixton prison, where his parents went to see him. On the first occasion, Mr Bentley noticed that one side of his son's face was badly bruised and that his nose was red and puffed. This had not been so at the magistrates' court. He asked Bentley what was the matter with his face. The warder who stood by during the visit stopped the conversation and told Mr Bentley that questions on the subject were not permitted. Did the father misrepresent the facts out of loyalty to his son? If not, had the warders been 'over-zealous' in their dealings with the prisoner? Nothing more was said or done about the matter. After all, there was not much sympathy for Derek Bentley in any quarter at the time. Even if he had been beaten up, a complaint might only make matters worse for him. His evidence of what he had said on the warehouse roof and in the car already contradicted the corroborated statements of police officers who were present on both occasions. If he added complaints of assault by the police or prison officers, with no witness to support these allegations either, would he not risk alienating a jury's belief in him totally?

The story of the case languished for only a day or two more. On Tuesday 11 November, nine days after the death of PC Miles, Christopher Craig was judged well enough to be taken from Croydon Hospital on a stretcher to the magistrates' court. With that, the story as reported by the press took on a new interest.

From this court appearance until after the Old Bailey trial, it was Craig who was the star attraction. Even when the case was over and the reporters were off the leash, Craig's story was the one that mattered. He had fired the gun. His unrepentant sardonic comments, regretting that he had not killed more or all of the policemen on the roof, had been reported at the preliminary hearing. Photographed on a stretcher, bandaged and wearing his blue dressing-gown, he looked moody and resentful, a Byronic child with a shock of dark hair. Here was the adolescent gunman, the incarnation of dedicated evil as the newspapers presented him. The public heard of his suicide bid, diving from the roof, and saw at their breakfast tables and on the commuter trains the photographs of wounded malevolence. There was a perverse or inverted glamour about him. Ten years earlier, such bravado as his in the face of superior numbers and the nonchalant suicide bid had been the stuff of romantic patriotism in underground resistance to a common enemy. Echoes of Special Operations Executive mingled with the thought that the boy in the newspaper photographs might have been almost anybody's son.

Bentley was largely forgotten. He was not the answer to a journalist's prayer. Craig, on the other hand, might be. At the end of the trial, the *Daily Herald* ran a feature on the two young criminals and on Norman Parsley, tried and sentenced the same day for his part with Craig in the armed robbery of Mr Howes, the Croydon greengrocer. All three were there, in words and photographs. Craig was the centrepiece. Even Parsley received more attention than Bentley. Bentley's blurred picture and story lay at one side of the main feature with a small caption: SENTENCED TO DEATH.

At Croydon magistrates' court on 11 November, Craig was carried from the ambulance. He had been brought to the building early, thirty-five minutes before the case was to be heard, in an attempt to avoid the crush of press and public in the street outside. But the spectators had been waiting long and patiently by that time. He was surrounded at once by uniformed police and a crowd of press photographers using flash-bulbs on the dull November day. By now the interest in the case was so great that the best photographs could only be taken from above. Before the trial was over, upstairs windows were hired by the press, ladders were used and, to give the best view to 'Sandy' Powell, the photographer was lifted by crane. The story was getting coverage in Europe and the Commonwealth. Interest in the United States was minimal. It was not just a matter of America's proverbial parochialism in such things. Craig and Bentley were small news compared with the murder-rate in American cities.

Craig's was a brief court appearance. He had nothing to say in answer to the charge of murder. The magistrates remanded him for a week and he was taken back to hospital. As he was being carried from the court, his father spoke to one of the officers. The stretcher was lowered long enough for Mrs Craig to stoop down, smile, and kiss her son. This was reported in the press next day as an example of what Archdeacon Tonks had called consideration for the wrongdoer at the expense of concern for his victim. Unsympathetic citizens wondered why Craig was being given pain-killing drugs when the desire of the nation was to cause him as much pain as possible.

The full details of the case against him did not come out at the first hearing before the magistrates. But the public had heard enough. Twelve uniformed policemen accompanied Chief Inspector John Smith as Craig was carried back to the ambulance. As they moved towards it, there was jostling in the crowd and shouts of 'Let's kill the little bastard!' Smith and his men held the line, keeping a path clear through the crowd. The stretcher was lifted into the ambulance, the doors slammed, and the vehicle nosed out through the crowds and traffic of central Croydon.

Between them, the Croydon onlookers and Archdeacon Tonks summed up the range of public reaction. Before the case was over, there were further suggestions that the law was at fault not in hanging Bentley at nineteen but in failing to hang Craig at sixteen. 'I think both little beggers ought to swing,' said Bentley's defence counsel Frank Cassels to Craig's counsel John Parris, when the two men met to discuss the case. To judge from the words and mood of the bystanders at Croydon magistrates' court, there would have been little opposition to such an expedient.

On the following Monday, 17 November, Craig appeared again

before the magistrates. This time the press reported a crowd of hundreds of people outside the building trying to get a glimpse of him. A fuller story was told by the witnesses. POLICE TELL OF GUN FIGHT WITH CRAIG, the papers reported next day, adding more of his remarks made in hospital for good measure. He was committed for trial at the Old Bailey and driven away by ambulance to wait on remand. This was the last time he was seen publicly outside the Old Bailey courtroom. 'Craig, dazzled by the photographers' flash-bulbs,' reported the *Daily Herald*, 'closed his eyes and grimaced as he was lifted into an ambulance that took him to Brixton Prison Hospital.' The final portrait of him in the press appeared to be of Craig pulling a face at the world in a farewell sneer of contempt.

On the same day, judges in Newcastle and Southend expressed a public wish that they could order the young offenders in front of them to be birched. That evening, a town meeting at Wimbledon under the patronage of two Conservative MPs, Sir Cyril Black and Sir Waldron Smithers, voted by a majority of thirty-to-one to urge the restoration of judicial flogging. Next morning the reports of all this were in the national press. Combined with shouts of 'Let's kill the little bastard!' from the Croydon crowd, such omens hardly seemed auspicious for the two youths who were about to be called to judgment. Unless an example were made of the culprits, there would surely be a public mood of the most bitter resentment against the administration of justice.

There was a further anxiety in the mind of the Home Secretary and many of his police officers. Craig was too young to hang, though he had committed the murder. He seemed bound to 'get away with it' on such grounds. What must the consequence be, if Bentley was shown mercy? A team of professional criminals need only recruit one ruthless and determined apprentice under the age of eighteen. If there were shooting to be done, let him do it. Even if the criminals were caught, the murderer's life would be safe. Unless the older members of the gang were made to understand that they would be held equally responsible for his act, what hope was there for a policeman or a civilian who got in their way? The issue was to be debated at greater length but it was already crucial to the argument.

While public attention remained on Craig, Bentley languished in Brixton prison. So far as he could comprehend the issues, he did so at the level of basic common sense and not at that of legal nicety. He had not carried a gun. It was possible that he did not know Craig was carrying one. He had not shot Miles nor attempted violence against anyone. That was in character, for he had no record of violence at all. He was not even sure when he climbed the side gate that there was to be a break-in at the warehouse. He and Craig were merely reconnoitring it after their failure at the butcher's shop and the electrical supplier. Moreover, he had been arrested by Fairfax when Miles was away from Tamworth Road, looking for the key-holder of the building. As a matter of law, he had been under arrest for at least quarter of an hour when the shot was fired that killed Miles. How could he be guilty of murdering a man who was nowhere around while Bentley was still at liberty and of whose very existence he was unaware? How could he be held responsible for Craig's actions when he was no longer in a position to influence them?

It still seemed that the charge of murder was a technicality, a figure of speech, not meant in earnest.

That apart, Craig and Bentley seemed a strangely ill-matched pair. The young and sardonic gunman, aggressive, quick, moody and resentful. The slow and dim-witted nineteen-year-old, physically awkward despite his height and body-building exercises, virtually unable to read or write, let alone to understand the legalities of his situation. Craig came from a home where the officer caste and a career in the professions were familiar concepts. Bentley's less privileged and less sophisticated family had struggled from ill-health and financial limitation to a place in the post-war security of South London. They had been twice bombed-out during the war. In one of these attacks a daughter, grandmother and aunt had been killed and in another Derek Bentley had been brought out from the wreckage in a state of shock. The Bentley parents had done their best for the children's education. Derek Bentley had been sent first to Sunday school and later to church.

It was almost a year before the murder of PC Miles, at about Christmas 1951, that Christopher Craig and Bentley first met. By then Bentley had been out of approved school for over a year and was working as a Croydon Corporation dustman. Their meeting may have been the result of Bentley having a girl-friend whose sister was the girl-friend of Craig. But in any case, his own sister Iris Bentley was also the friend of a girl going out with Craig.

Both boys had criminal convictions. Craig had left school that year and had just been fined at Hove for having a Webley .45 revolver without a licence. This was the only offence with which he had ever been charged. In 1948, Bentley had twice appeared before Croydon magistrates. On the first occasion he was bound over for trying to break into a shop and also for attempting to steal some small change and tickets from a bus conductor's bag. On the second occasion Bentley and another boy had been caught playing with tools on a building site. They were convicted of stealing the tools, though Bentley's father insisted that there was no evidence that the tools had been stolen at all, let alone by his son. One of the magistrates asked Bentley to spell the word 'fluorescent'. He could not even read it, let alone spell it. In consequence of this, he was sentenced to three years in an approved school, though released after less than two.

As in so many instances before magistrates' courts, the decision did little to enhance the reputation of those who made it. The social freemasonry of how and why magistrates were appointed was not open to question. They were there as if by Act of God, and usually by virtue of political patronage or personal connection. Not surprisingly, they showed little sympathy for the case put forward on Bentley's behalf. However, the authorities had him examined at the time by Dr James Munroe of the Department of Psychological Medicine at Guys Hospital. Dr Munroe reported that the boy was feeble-minded and suffered from epilepsy.

The development of the friendship between Craig and their son, from Christmas 1951 until November 1952, was to be described almost entirely from the viewpoint of the Bentley family. To that extent it was partisan. Yet no one could reasonably doubt that it was Craig who exercised intelligence and influence, for Bentley was ill-equipped with either.

According to Mr Bentley, on the very first occasion that Craig and Derek Bentley met, Craig talked about 'jobs' that he had 'pulled.' Not surprisingly, if that were the case, the Bentley parents warned their son against this new acquaintance and did their best to keep him from Craig's company and example. They suggested that Bentley himself was a reluctant companion of the younger boy but that Craig persisted in the association. Bentley's sister, working as an usherette at the Streatham Astoria, recalled that she used to see her brother come in alone. Presently Craig would follow him, as if not to be shaken off. So far as criminal enterprise was concerned, Bentley seems an odd choice of partner. In the case of the Tamworth Road warehouse, he was of no use whatever to Craig. Indeed, he proved to be a liability when it came to moving silently in the dark or climbing to the roof.

It was in May 1952 that the police first made a connection between the two. Some empty petrol cans had been found at the end of the Bentleys' garden. Derek Bentley, Craig and one of their friends were summoned to Norbury police station for questioning. There was no valid evidence against them and no charge was brought. However, Sergeant Reed came out and delivered what he called 'a friendly word of warning' to Mr Bentley, in his son's presence, in the police station waiting-room. He warned Mr Bentley to keep Derek away from Craig.

Derek Bentley protested that he had no wish to see Craig but found it impossible to get away from him. Sergeant Reed advised him to ignore his shadow. Just ignore him.

This was easier said than done. Again, though the story continued to be told from the Bentleys' point of view, the boy's father felt increasing cause for alarm. If his son was not Craig's friend, might he not become his enemy? A week before the death of PC Miles, there was an incident at Fairview Road. According to Mr Bentley, his worst fears were confirmed and he was back at Norbury police station on Monday morning, 27 October, asking to see Sergeant Reed.

There was to be an annual dance for employees of the Rank

Organisation, including Iris Bentley. The friend who asked her to get tickets was also the girl-friend of Craig. It was Craig who came to Fairview Road on Sunday 26 October to collect the tickets. While he was at the Bentleys' house, Craig was alleged by Mr Bentley to have said, 'If anyone dances with my girl, I'll go for them with my knife.' He went over to Derek Bentley and reminded him that the threat applied to him as well. In Mr Bentley's account, Craig said to Derek Bentley, 'Watch your step. You've got it coming to you.'

Even if true, it was possible that such words might have been spoken as adolescent bravado, a ritual display of male aggression in the mating game. They might even have been said as a sardonic joke. However, Mr Bentley recalled that he was sufficiently alarmed at the threat to his son to go to Norbury police station next morning and seek out Sergeant Reed. He gave an account of the conversation at Fairview Road the previous day. And then he asked that Craig should in some way be restrained from waylaying his son. The police should offer Derek Bentley some protection against the threats that were being made by his unwanted friend.

Perhaps the notion of a nineteen-year-old in good physical shape from body-building having to be protected from a sixteen-year-old seemed absurd. At any rate, Sergeant Reed explained that Craig did not appear to be breaking any law and that his 'antics' were beyond any power of the police to check.

'What do you expect us to do?' he asked.

Mr Bentley suggested that the police might give Craig a warning of some kind. But there was nothing, ostensibly, to warn him about. So, according to Mr Bentley, the sergeant promised that the local police would keep an eye on Craig. With that, the matter was at an end.

Subsequently, Mr Bentley through his amanuensis recalled that, 'I felt rather small as I walked back home. But I never had the slightest doubt that Craig was a danger to the people in the district.'

Later that week, Niven Craig was tried at the Old Bailey and the March armed robbery at Waltham Abbey became public news. Whether the Norbury police made any connection between this and Christopher Craig is uncertain. As yet, it seems that the Bentley family had remained in ignorance of Niven Craig's story or the sympathy and resentment felt by the younger brother in respect of the elder and those who had brought him to justice. With that, the two families were engulfed in the darker drama of the Croydon shooting.

The press, by hindsight, painted a lurid picture of the 'Craig Gang' and its activities in the Croydon area. The title was devised by the *Daily Herald* on 12 December, in a feature called CRAIG'S GIRL FRIENDS WERE GIVEN JEWELS. By this means, girls as young as thirteen were transformed for the public imagination into gangsters' molls, glittering with 'ice' and wrapped in white mink. The oldest member of the gang was said to be twenty-two. 'Craig had quite a following. Four or five other boys – and a few girls... They met in local cinemas and cafés. Sometimes there were presents of jewellery for the girls. Craig dominated the meetings. Bentley, sentenced with him for the murder, was his chief lieutenant.'

The symbols were all there: the gunmen and their girls, the jewels and the presents, the meetings and the leader who dominated the others. No one could fault it as fantasy. It was the reality that let it down. Whether any self-respecting gang would have tolerated Craig's leadership, judged by the proceeds of his crimes, seems doubtful. Four pounds from the elderly greengrocer and nothing at all in Tamworth Road. Suspicion of knocking off a can of petrol. It was hardly Chicago-style or Chicago-scale, despite the zanier Fleet Street fantasies. Bentley as the gang-leader's lieutenant was even more improbable. His known haul was less than a pound from a bus-conductor's pouch when he was fifteen. The keys to the butcher's shop had proved useless. His most distinctive contribution to the warehouse raid had been kicking over a dustbin and getting stuck on a drainpipe.

Meetings in the cinemas and cafés of Croydon or Streatham suggested anything but a crime syndicate. It was how most people of that age met in public on most occasions, unless the place chosen was a dance-hall. The better-looking girls from Broad

Green Grammar School and other private schools showed off at Streatham Ice-Rink, supervised and safe from the 'gang' and its attentions. All the same, the adherence of girls from the third or fourth forms of local schools to the syndicate suggests Just William or Bugsy Malone rather than Al Capone or Machine-Gun Kelly.

But of such unpromising material a legend was fashioned, in the days before and after the Old Bailey trial. It added a certain spice to the breakfast-table reading of Fleet Street's customers to know that the girls were as bad as the boys in their way. The press reported the case of a girl of twelve, described by the judge as 'A Menace'. Was there not the 'cosh-girl' waiting with firetongs for the returning pensioner? It was almost unsporting to suggest the truth, that the elderly as a group were statistically less likely to be victims of crime than their juniors. Even when crime struck them, they were more at risk from the amateur pilfering of devious schoolchildren, not from the violent attentions of professional villains.

But it was not the truths of statistics in which the newspapers dealt. Whatever the figures might say, the drama of individual suffering was the stuff of breakfast reading. Truth was individual, not general. Reading such stories, men and women echoed the sentiments of Archdeacon Tonks. 'This is not England, the England we have known and for which men and women have laid down their lives.'

In that case, what had gone wrong? More than four centuries earlier, in 1531, in his *Boke Named the Governour*, Sir Thomas Elyot contended that the 'braines and hertes of children' were open to the evil influence of 'some pestiferous dewe of vice,' whose example might 'infecte and corrupt the softe and tender buddes.' Men and women who had never heard of Elyot or his book would now have agreed with him unhesitatingly. The conduct of the young in the early 1950s seemed proof of his assertion. There had been 'evil custome' for example. Even in the weeks before Craig and Bentley came to trial, a good deal of debate and writing was devoted to identifying just where and how that example had been allowed to flourish.

CHAPTER 8

Bewildered by the apparent growth of armed robbery and violent crime in the seven years since the end of the war, the nation and its judges sought explanations and remedies.

Yet the problem of a post-war crime-wave was more familiar in England than commentators of the day usually cared to admit. At an equally momentous time, a letter from the Prime Minister's son to a close friend reported 'little news from England but of robberies.' With the war's end, demobilised servicemen took to the streets with violent intent, so that 'people are almost afraid of stirring after it is dark.' In 1952, Archbishop Tonks and the *Daily Mail*, Lord Chief Justice Goddard and the British Housewives League made precisely that point. Robbery and violence, wrote the same Prime Minister's son, were so common that the forces of law in the capital could no longer keep pace with the incidents. And this was true. Armed hold-ups during broad day were common in Westminster itself. As it happens, the author of that letter was Horace Walpole writing in 1749 to his friend Sir Horace Mann. The War of the Austrian Succession to which he refers had been ended in the previous year by the Treaty of Aix-la-Chapelle. That particular crime-wave had been infinitely more terrifying than anything known in London during the twentieth century.

But it was little comfort to the readers of the *Daily Telegraph* or the *Daily Mirror*, two hundred years later, to know that armed robbery and violence had been as bad after the peace treaty of 1748, or 1815, or 1919. They knew only that their own families might be confronted at dead of night by armed and masked intruders. The cosh and the gun-butt, the tying into chairs and ripping out of telephones, the questions and beating, the wrecking and robbing of their homes, were the familiar small change of Hollywood gangsterdom.

But so far as the public imagined the police in 1952 fighting against a rising tide of crime, it was wrong. Metropolitan crime had risen during the latter half of the war, when much of London and England seemed like a vast military transit camp. From 1945 until 1950, the crime rate declined steadily and the detection rate rose. Throughout the year of the Derek Bentley and Christopher Craig case – and into the following year – there was again a decline in crimes committed. As Sir Harold Scott, Commissioner of Metropolitan Police, pointed out, the crimes of murder and manslaughter were no more common than they had been before the war. The most serious increase was in sexual offences, particularly homosexual conduct which was later removed from the category of crime, and crimes of wounding, which were between thirty and forty per cent higher than they had been in the 1930s. Most of the increase in crimes of wounding, however, was not the consequence of gang-battles or robberies, but of family quarrels.

For all that, the spectre of the masked gunman seemed more frequent, and there was reason to think that the police were particularly at risk. For that state of affairs, the war and the attitude of the young could plausibly be held responsible.

Horace Walpole's highwayman of two centuries before, no less than the urban gangster of 1952, had used a gun and a mask. But the mass-production of weapons for vast conscript armies and the easy ownership of pistols by individuals had created a gun-culture in the 1920s. Famous cases of the decade seemed to show that. Ronald True, the ex-officer and gentleman, shot dead the girl he robbed in 1922, whereas a Victorian or Edwardian cad might have bludgeoned her to death. In the celebrated case of Madame Fahmy, revenging herself for the sodomy which her husband committed upon her at the Savoy Hotel in 1923, the gun took the place of poison, which had been the traditional 'woman's weapon' of Victorian crime. Petty gangsters like Browne and Kennedy in 1927 shot dead the policeman who stood in their way. As in the 1920s, so in the 1940s. The so-called 'Cleft-Chin Murder' was the most talked of London case during the Second World War. Once again, it was a gun in the hands of a US Army deserter and the complicity of his English striptease-dancer girl-friend which gave reality a touch of Peter Cheyney or James Hadley Chase. In 1947 the murder of Alec de Antiquis in an attempted jewel robbery, against a background of gun-shots in a busy London street, became the criminal sensation of the year. Two men were hanged for the killing. And once again it was all for nothing. The gang had come away empty-handed.

There was a further cause for concern after the Second World War. The availability of guns, including automatic weapons, was far greater in the years after 1945 than it had been after 1918. From the abandoned stockpiles of the defeated Reich and the discarded equipment of the Allies, the professional criminals furnished their arsenals. 'Just after the war,' wrote Sir Harold Scott in 1954, 'large numbers of firearms were being brought to this country by servicemen from overseas theatres of war. Strict measures of control and search in Germany and other places and at the ports of arrival quickly put a stop to this traffic.'

But not quickly enough to prevent Christopher Craig at sixteen from having owned forty guns at one time or another. Access to firearms was more widespread than mere looting of enemy stockpiles for souvenirs. When a post-war amnesty was announced, some 30,000 guns were surrendered to the police. But even after that, from personal experience, it was possible at the time of the Craig and Bentley case for a schoolboy to buy an 'obsolete' pistol from an antique or 'curio' shop. As a weapon, it was inaccurate at any distance. On the other hand, it could be made to fire a metal ball which, at point blank range against a wall, would blow a hole the size of a finger-joint in the plaster and brickwork. Far more important, this was the sort of improvisation that was to lead to the murder with which Derek Bentley and Christopher Craig were charged. Craig's .455 Eley service revolver was not a modern gun but a weapon of the 1914–18 war. He worked upon it and filed down ammunition of different calibre so that the rounds would fit what he liked to call proudly but wrongly his 'Colt .45.'

Restrictions on the sale of lesser weapons scarcely existed at all. Loaded canes or coshes were advertised in shop windows. Until the outbreak of war, the British National Socialist League had organised the open sale of daggers and coshes from shops sympathetic to its political aims, in order to arm Fascists for the world struggle. Knuckledusters were stocked by certain ironmongers, though Craig made his own at the garage where he worked as a fitter after leaving school. In the light of this, the Victorian tradition of an Englishman's healthy reliance on his own fists and strength seemed decidedly antiquated.

Even a ban on the sale of such implements would do nothing to prevent the improvised weaponry of the kitchen knife or the razor-blade embedded in a potato. But in the years after 1945 it was the gun which represented status and power. To some commentators it was seen as a symbol of the new criminal generation. To the young men who lived with its presence, it had a more direct and useful justification.

The more distant forebears of Derek Bentley and Christopher Craig in using guns against the police were ex-servicemen like Frederick Browne and William Kennedy, two robbers hanged in 1928 for the shooting of a policeman in Essex while they were in possession of a stolen car. Petty and unsuccessful thieves otherwise, like Bentley and Craig, their crime was redolent of a new type of gangster with his weapons and getaway vehicles. In the fifty years before 1952, sixteen policemen were murdered on duty in England and Wales. All but two were shot. The true significance of this, in stirring up public apprehension, was that a quarter of all these deaths, as well as another murder of a policeman by shooting in Scotland, had occurred within two years before the crime of Derek Bentley and Christopher Craig. Another such killing was almost added to the list. Though Niven Craig had not shot Detective-Sergeant Lewis in the Bayswater bedroom, he had evidently been prepared to do so.

It was not enough to point out that the number of actual police murders was still very small, a minute figure in proportion to the number of policemen killed in the United States. It was the nature of each case, the outrage or the tragedy as the press reported it,

that made the greater impact on the British public. So long as one policeman's widow grieved for a murdered husband, the problem was of national importance. Indeed, such a principle was provided for in the special protection which English law traditionally gave to officers of justice.

As it happened, the nature of the threat which Craig and his kind posed to society was more alarming than its scale. In 1951 and 1952, five policemen had been killed on duty in England and Wales, and one in Scotland. All but one of them had died by shooting. Yet, though it was no comfort to potential victims and their families, the appearance of guns in the Metropolitan Police area – or any other part of the United Kingdom – was comparatively rare and their actual use still rarer. Between 1945 and 1953, the Commissioner of Metropolitan Police reported that two of his officers, including Miles, had been shot dead. The figure for the United States had been sixty-four in 1951 alone. This was something like eight times as many, per head of the population.

Even the use of guns in other crimes was more frightening than frequent. Between 1945 and 1952, for example, the number of armed robberies in London had begun at forty-six a year. As in Niven Craig's case, guns were carried almost always to threaten rather than to fire. Such cases dropped sharply to nineteen for the year in 1950, and were the same in 1952. In the latter year, the two offences by the Craig brothers alone respresented more than a tenth of all armed robbery among the capital's eight million people. The trouble with statistics for crimes that were so infrequent was that one or two determined villains or bullying adolescents could produce the most alarming figures

Indisputably, the ultimate crime of such guns was murder. Yet, even so, most murderers had nothing to do with firearms. Among the more sensational killings of the post-war years, Neville Heath had used a penknife on one occasion, a whip and a pillow on another. Daniel Raven used a television aerial to batter Mrs Goodman in 1949. Harry Lewis hit Harry Michaelson with a tubular steel chair. Even the most elaborate murder of all, when Donald Hume dropped the dismembered and parcelled body of

Stanley Setty from an aeroplane over the Thames estuary, had apparently been carried out with a simple kitchen-knife.

It would have been unthinkable to belittle any act of murder or violence, yet the publicity gained by it produced a distorted view of Metropolitan crime. The prospect of unarmed police facing a Chicago-style epidemic of gunmen on the loose was misleading. In the Metropolitan area, such crimes appear to have been perpetrated by a couple of dozen men in a population of eight million, a good many of the criminals already being known to the police from other causes. But the fear of a rising tide of armed crime was real enough. Sir Harold Scott, as Commissioner of Metropolitan Police, remarked at the time that a good many law-abiding applicants for firearms certificates wished to have 'a weapon for their personal protection at home and are apprehensive because of what they have read about attacks on householders... but if it were common for householders to be armed there would be a real danger that the thieves would shoot their way in and out after the manner of a gangster film.' Herbert Morrison, as Home Secretary, had shared this fear. He had suggested to all chief police officers, 'a very strict policy in granting certificates'.

In an age of instant television news and comment, backed up by a growing concentration of power in the mass circulation press, the case of Craig and Bentley was one of the first to focus and distort public concern on such a scale. To sell newspapers and hold a television audience, a single topic must be boosted, exploited, then dropped in favour of another. In the late 1980s, a child is far more likely to be killed or seriously injured by a drunken, careless or arrogant motorist than by sexual abuse. But themes of child abuse or child pornography may be pursued and purveyed with an ambiguous enthusiasm, raising circulation or viewing figures. Avoidable deaths and injuries of children on the roads may be a hundred-fold more frequent, even the past wisdom of marketing cars with names like 'Avenger' and 'Hunter' might be questioned. But that is not the chosen topic of the day. Space or time given to it would dilute the appeal of the preferred theme in which time and money have been invested. The functioning of mass media requires that public concern should be trained to the current issue. So, in the early 1950s, the gunman and the street-gang, the Teddy Boy and the dance-hall razor-fight, became the catalyst of moral comment.

Few people accord the press or television anything like the respect which those institutions accord themselves. Indeed, the decreasing attention-span of moral concern on the part of professional commentators would matter much less, were it not for its final stage. This is the conclusion – and the demand – that 'something must be done' about whatever the scandal and the problem may be. A law must be passed or an example made. There must be a calling to account. It was precisely this demand, common to such secular evangelising for the past thirty or forty years, that was to cost Derek Bentley his life.

Ironically, in the light of the preoccupation with the figure of the gunman, there is no evidence that Bentley had ever carried a firearm, let alone used one or knew how to. Both Craig and Bentley carried knives. Craig threatened to use his, according to Mr Bentley. But the folklore of the day, gleaned from crime comic and cinema screen, was wiser than the examples of reality. The criminal was increasingly seen as the gangster. The gangster had been a gunman for quarter of a century. When children played at cops and robbers, they did not usually pretend to stab or cut. They said, 'Bang! Bang! You're dead.' And increasingly, it seemed, they said it in earnest.

CHAPTER 9

Guns were merely the instruments of crime, not its motivation. What kind of 'evil example', to use Sir Thomas Elyot's phrase, had brought the morals of the rising generation to such a pass? Lack of parental control and the 'breakdown' of family life was an easy answer. But those who employed it always intended that it should be other families than their own who stood accused. And, in the case of both Craig and Bentley, the suggestion seemed entirely erroneous. Both, as children, had been under the influence of Sunday school, Bible class, and church. Six of the eight Craig children were among life's successes. Their parents had encouraged their educational and moral development. Of the two errant brothers, Niven Craig's true teenage delinquency began when the army took him over. Had the warehouse gate in Tamworth Road proved impregnable, Christopher Craig's year of guns and bravado might still have ended as an adolescent phase.

It was outside the family that the teenage culture of the 1950s had firmest hold. The café and the dance-hall, the cinema and the paperback novel, the children's comic and even the bland output of television took their share of the blame. The impact of books, films and comics seemed to affect sons rather than daughters. If parents feared for their girls' innocence, it was the dance-hall and the jazz club that gave them most concern.

This was the age of Ronnie Scott's and the crowded clubs where those jazz fans who danced instead of coming to listen were packed together in unavoidable intimacy. Soon it was also the decade of 'Elvis the Pelvis' with suggestive hip-gyrations, and guitars angled with phallic self-confidence. Leader-writers in *The Times* had been apt, in their old-fashioned way, to see the path to national decadence through the sexual looseness of the dance-floor. 'National morals depend on national habits', wrote one of them, 'It is quite sufficient to cast one's eyes on the voluptuous intertwining of the limbs, and close compression of the bodies in this dance... So long as this obscene display was confined to prostitutes and adulteresses, we did not think it deserving of notice, but... we feel it a duty to warn every parent against exposing his daughter to so fatal a contagion.'

As in the case of Horace Walpole's gunmen, it was refreshing to know that the date of publication of this leading article was long past, 16 July 1816, and that the dance whose sexual immorality shocked more profoundly than jazz clubs or rock and roll was, of course, the waltz.

Far more disturbing than sexual suggestiveness in books, films and comics, were crime and violence, because they were more freely portrayed. Particularly the violence of the gun. The gun played some part in almost every cinema double-bill for the over-sixteens ('A' Certificate). But long before Hollywood, the tradition of melodrama coupled violence or crime with a preacher's morality. The truth of 'Murder will out' or even 'Thou shalt not kill', was portrayed as intensely on the screen as from the pulpit. That crime did not pay was the message of lurid melodrama like *Maria Marten, or Murder in the Old Red Barn* a century earlier, in the *Newgate Calendar* fifty years before that, even four centuries earlier in the rogue-histories of the first Elizabethan Age, like Thomas Nashe's *The Unfortunate Traveller* (1594). When, in the 1960s, part of Nashe's novel was to be read out on stage as part of a production at the Oxford Playhouse, the Lord Chamberlain stepped in and banned it. There was, it seemed, little that the crime comics could have taught the first Elizabethans.

A gentler tone was evident in much public entertainment of the mid-twentieth century. The two most accomplished westerns, *Destry Rides Again* (1939) and *High Noon* (1952) made a virtue of their heroes' abhorrence of guns – coupled with extreme proficiency in their use. The peace-loving defender of the innocent who was reluctantly goaded to conflict and heroism by his evil enemy had been, after all, the Allies' moral posture in the Second World War. In the game of cowboys and Indians, there was an improved moral example in films like John Ford's *She Wore a Yellow Ribbon* (1949), where the object was to avert an Indian rising rather than to suppress it in a massacre of anonymous hordes.

Among the most distinguished gangster films of the British post-war period, Carol Reed's *Odd Man Out* in 1946 or *Brighton Rock* in the following year did little for the image of the gunman. A tragic figure in the first and a failed devil in the second, there was much to pity and little to emulate. The gun acquired its true significance only when the hero could kill and feel good about it because he represented law, justice, morality, or when those gunned down were his country's enemies.

So, for example, the sombre and dissuasive role of the gun in Howard Hawks' film of Raymond Chandler's *The Big Sleep* in 1946 was balanced by Alan Ladd in *O.S.S.* parachuting into France before D-Day and dealing with the Nazi occupiers as they deserved. Patriotism and pride in military victory made it unthinkable that the guns of the Second World War should fall silent on the screen. Those who were most vocal in deploring the lawless young men were also first in their enthusiasm for celebrating the memory of that Finest Hour. Even before the case of Craig and Bentley was over, Gilbert Harding, homespun and irrascible on the television screen, had denounced the young for being 'spoon-fed and spineless', by contrast with those who had gone out and fought the Hun. The Craig brothers must have thought they had done their best to prove him wrong.

The moral vigilantes spoke and wrote as if the nation lay helpless in the path of a tide of cinema violence. As it happened, films were subject to a degree of censorship which other countries and other decades found intolerable. It was open to the British Board of Film Censors to ban or categorise films as they chose. A few films were banned outright, as was the case with *The Wild Ones*. Starring Marlon Brando and Lee Marvin, this was made at the time of the Bentley and Craig case. Its story of a motor-cycle gang raising hell in a small town was precisely the example to be kept from the eyes and minds of England's youth after the Croydon shooting. Films were otherwise categorised as 'U,' 'A,' and 'X.' Universal certificates made them freely available. Adult certificates excluded children under sixteen unless accompanied by an adult. 'X' certificates excluded all those under eighteen and had lately replaced the old 'H' or Horror certificates, dating from the days of *King Kong* and *Frankenstein*, whose first showing reputedly caused swoonings and dead-faints.

Until 1952, however, censorship in England and the United States meant principally the vetting of sexual content. Indeed, producers and directors were self-censors in the first place. In Chandler's novel of *The Big Sleep*, Arthur Geiger's speciality is hiring pornography from the back room of his Los Angeles book store. Carmen Sternwood is compromised when photographed naked in his house. By the time that the story reached the screen, there was no indication that pornography featured in the plot at all and Carmen Sternwood was photographed fully dressed. In the Chandler novel *Farewell, My Lovely*, Philip Marlowe is kissing young Mrs Grayle, 'her tongue was a darting snake between her teeth,' when her elderly husband enters the room. In the 1945 film, Mrs Grayle offers him no more than a significant glance and it is her step-daughter who comes into the room.

To protect the Bentley and Craig generation from their own worst instincts, the British film censor's scissors hovered over such improbable subjects as the costume drama *Forever Amber* and the toned-down film version of James Hadley Chase's thriller *No Orchids for Miss Blandish*. Howard Hughes' western *The Outlaw* was held up until 1946, largely because of a publicity-still which showed Jane Russell's bosom about to spill out of her blouse, a picture which did not appear in the film anyway. The effect of *No Orchids for Miss Blandish* in its film version was undermined from the start by a cast of English actors assuming questionable American accents. The appearance in this underworld of familiar faces like Sid James and Jack La Rue – of the Jack La Rue and Monty Blue comedy duo – was apt to raise chuckles in the cinema rather than a chill down the spine.

As for fiction, the suppression of books was acquiring an ill fame. The so-called 'Purification Bonfires' of the Third Reich had shown literary censorship in its worst light. England's pre-war prosecutions of publishers for such books as the *Satyricon* of Petronius Arbiter or Radclyffe Hall's *The Well of Loneliness* appeared as legal and moral absurdities by 1952. The new Labour government dithered as to whether or not to prosecute in respect of Kathleen Winsor's historical novel *Forever Amber*, a feeble and fancy-dress *Moll Flanders*. The failure of prosecutions in the United States courts secured the publication of the book in England. In Boston, Judge Frank J. Donahue had described it as 'a soporific rather than an aphrodisiac... conducive to sleep... not conducive to sleep with a member of the opposite sex.' In May 1949, the Attorney-General, Sir Hartley Shawcross, told the House of Commons that he had also decided to take no action in respect of another American best-seller, Norman Mailer's graphic and gruesome novel of war, *The Naked and the Dead*.

So far as murder and gangsterdom were concerned, British publishers and their authors knew the limits of toleration and usually observed them. In 1942 there had been an obscenity prosecution and suppression of James Hadley Chase's novel, *Miss Callaghan Comes to Grief*. In the cultural 'crack down' that followed the Craig and Bentley case, fifty-two destruction orders were obtained for the crime novels of 'Hank Janson' in 1954. In the following year, in a trial almost without modern precedent outside a totalitarian regime, D. F. Crawley, the original author of 'Hank Janson,' was prosecuted for having written the novels. He was acquitted when it was discovered that he had sold the pen-name some time before. It is a measure of the growing hysteria, however, that no one in the service of the Treasury Solicitor or the Director of Public Prosecutions had bothered to check this before wasting public time and money on a futile case.

There was one hard-boiled crime novel that proved too much for the censors, then and now. It came from France, where the distinguished novelist Boris Vian also wrote crime fiction as 'Vincent Sullivan,' books which Vian claimed to have 'translated from the American.' The French best-seller of 1947 was Vincent Sullivan's *J'Irai Cracher Sur Vos Tombes*, translated as *I'll Spit on Your Graves*. It was at once put on the 'stop-list' of British customs officials, whose waterguard branch rated it the most offensive of the books on their reading-list.

Books, as opposed to films and comics, were of little direct interest to Bentley or Craig. Bentley's reading age remained that of a child of four and a half. Craig feared being asked to read aloud at his Bible class and making a fool of himself. His father later gave evidence in court that his son could manage 'small words,' presumably enough to get him through a children's comic.

Had the ideas and attitudes of post-war crime fiction percolated into the comics and the films? It was hard for the nation's educators not to be disturbed by certain episodes in such novels as *No Orchids for Miss Blandish* or Mickey Spillane's *I, the Jury*. Spillane's novel, published in the year of the Bentley and Craig case, is the story of Mike Hammer's search for the murderer of a friend, shot in the stomach and left to die in agony. The precise agony of such a death is elaborated for use later in the book. On the last page the killer is revealed as the beautiful Charlotte Manning, who undresses slowly in front of Hammer, unaware that he is about to kill her in the same way. 'Her hands hooked in the fragile silk of her panties and pulled them down. She stepped out of them as delicately as one coming from a bath-tub... The roar of the .45 shook the room. Charlotte staggered back a step. Her eyes were a symphony of incredulity, an unbelieving witness to the truth. Slowly she looked down at the ugly swelling in her naked belly where the bullet went in. A thin trickle of blood welled out... "How c-could you?" she gasped. I only had a moment before talking to a corpse, but I got it in. "It was easy," I said.'

The book ends at that point, blending a sardonic enjoyment of vengeance, erotic provocation, carefully savoured cruelty, and a pernicious feeling of moral righteousness. The amused contempt shown to the dying victim was a hallmark of the genre, as when Slim in *No Orchids for Miss Blandish* pins Riley to a tree by driving a knife through his stomach, lights a cigarette and leaves him to his final agony with the words, 'Take your time, pal.' But in Spillane's novels, sadism becomes a civic duty. In *One Lonely Night*, also published in England in the year of the Craig and Bentley case, Mike Hammer's mission is to fight for what he calls 'Mr and Mrs Average People' against the menace of Communist subversion, 'the same outfit that tried to make a mockery of our courts and who squirmed into the government and tried to bring it down around our necks.' The scandal of Senator McCarthy's investigations of un-American activities had yet to rebound on the inquisitors. Righteous America could cheer on Mike Hammer, in 1952, as he revelled in gunning down the Communist gang. 'They were Red sons-of-bitches who should have died long ago, and part of the gang who are going to be dying in the very near future unless they get smart and take the gas pipe. Pretty soon what's left of Russia and the slime that breeds there won't be worth mentioning and I'm glad because I had a part in the killing.'

However self-defeating censorship may be in the end, it seems extraordinary that those who 'cleaned up' and 'cracked down' glared at Chase and smiled on Spillane. But, after all, during the Second World War the bloodshed in the comic strips that alarmed the 1950s had been a patriotic stimulus when the 'Krauts' and the 'Nips' were on the receiving end. Even comic strips for infants had cartoon characters like 'Musso da Wop – He's a bigga-da Flop.' Ten years later, the moral vigilantes in England and the United States overlooked Spillane who, after all, was on our side against a godless Soviet enemy. So wicked and naked young women might be shot in the stomach and left to die in agony. As the Korean war became a world struggle, 'Russia and the slime that breeds there' was to get its desserts. Nor did the criminals at home fare better. In *The Long Wait*, Hammer kills one opponent who has an arm in plaster, first putting the good arm over a table and breaking it, then breaking the other one 'all over again.' Another moral deviant is nailed to the floor to prevent his escape, 'Better 'n handcuffs, buddy.' Like the comic-book heroes of the Second World War, Mike Hammer had justice on his side as a Cold War warrior and protector of 'Mr and Mrs Average People' in the 1950s. His strength was that he, in their fantasies, did what many contemporaries would have liked to see done to thugs and gunmen in reality.

America took little notice of the Craig and Bentley case, with one exception. In 1954, Dr Frederick Wertheim produced his book, *The Seduction of the Innocent*, which became something of a cult among educationalists. Its thesis was that the ills of contemporary childhood and adolescence came from the habit of reading comics. All comics were the object of attack, but particularly *Superman* and crime comics.

The Seduction of the Innocent was a crusade rather than a scientific investigation. Read the first time, it shocks as a polemic. Read the second time, its argument lies open to doubt. If it fails to convince, that is perhaps because too much second-hand information, 'Camp counsellors have told me that...' is taken at face-value and too much of the indictment depends on Dr Wertheim's verbal description and interpretation of selected visual material, which the reader does not see. The children in his care were for the most part delinquent or deprived in some way, so that whether their crime comic reading was the cause or effect of this is not established. Like many enthusiasts for a theory, he sees life in terms of it, often writing as if the world consisted exclusively of children and adolescents reading crime comics. Nothing is said of the effect of America's public life on the young. The popular enthusiasm, for example, attending the ritual and details of capital punishment, the chair, the gallows, the gas-chamber, or the playgrounds where children counted down to the hour when a well-advertised judicial killing was to take place. And in an extraordinary piece of special pleading or volte-face, Dr Wertheim brushes aside criticism of the novels of former comic-book writer Mickey Spillane as 'sheer hypocrisy.'

Dr Wertheim presents Craig as a boy whose crimes were directly related to the comics he read. 'Who can say that the crime would have occurred if this boy's reading disability had been cured early and he had been given decent literature to read instead of these comic books?' In other words, the argument is circular and self-defeating. 'Who can say that if the world were different, it would not be different?' The unsurprising facts are that comics in England were overwhelmingly English with some American imports. The *Beano* and the *Dandy*, *Film Fun* and *Radio Fun* had been the staple diet during the years of Craig's childhood. The amiable smiles of George Formby and Arthur Askey presided where Mike Hammer might later have run riot. Desperate Dan,

Pansy Potter the Strong Man's Daughter, and Freddie the Fearless Fly peopled the strips of Craig's infancy. There was, to be sure, a syndicated story from America in which the heroine was tied on her back by the villain with her legs apart, so that a circular-saw might run slowly between her thighs and divide her inch by inch. The possibilities were suggestive and horrific, though the hero arrived to rescue her at the last moment. The doomed heroine was Claribel Cow, the dog-faced villain was Peg-Leg Pete and the rescuer was Mickey Mouse, in whose *Mickey Mouse Weekly* the nail-biting drama unfolded.

Even so, a vague reference during the murder trial to comics said little about Craig's taste in literature, violent or otherwise. It was the second part of his father's answer, omitted by Dr Wertheim, that gave the game away. Unable to read himself, the boy liked other people to read aloud to him. His choice fell exclusively on one author, Enid Blyton. Her determinedly moralistic tales for younger children were 'the only books he knows anything about.' If there was a purely literary influence on the crime in Tamworth Road, the creator of Noddy and the Famous Five seemed to be a prime candidate. After that the matter of literature and its 'evil example' on Craig was dropped.

'Books copy life,' wrote Théophile Gautier in 1835, 'Life doesn't copy books.' However debatable, it contained one truth in the case of Craig and Bentley that all the talk about films and comics overlooked.

For six years, from 1939 until 1945, the guns and the bombs of the righteous had been officially designated as cleansing and liberating. For much of that time, the authorities in most of Europe had been the enemy, the German occupiers. Among the elite of the forces of freedom were the commando groups and resistance fighters who gunned down the uniformed representatives of Nazi law and order. Captain W. E. Johns, long famous as the author of 'Biggles,' created a new set of characters for a series of commando adventures led by 'Gimlet' King, in *King of the Commandos* and its sequels. The deaths of Germans in occupied France by sten-gun and even bow-and-arrow were offered for the admiration of the young. As Sir Harold Scott pointed out after the war, it was not those who had served in the commandos who took to crime in disproportionate numbers, but their admirers who adapted the spirit of an armed elite for their own criminal gratification.

When Captain Johns set pen to paper, he was reflecting and not creating a public attitude to the world conflict. Even by 1952, the example of a righteous war was too recent to be easily set aside. Had Bentley and Craig, a decade before the murder with which they were charged, refused to carry and fire a gun in their country's service, they would at least have faced a tribunal and possibly a prison sentence. To inscribe a sardonic message on the nose of a bomb that might wipe out an ordinary family in Hamburg or Berlin had been fair game. It was even amusing, in its way, doing to them what they had done to us. As a gesture, it belonged in the world of 'Take your time, pal,' or ' "It was easy," I said.'

It was not to be disputed that war against the evil of the Third Reich had been necessary, its overthrow the only hope for the salvation of Europe. But the psychological price of victory was seldom acknowledged. Indeed, it was seldom anticipated that there would be such a price. 'After the war' was to be the world of the New Jerusalem, where dreams came true and the people lived happily ever after. But an entire nation had known the exhilaration and apprehension of the world struggle. The sten-gun and the commando-attack had been symbols to set the adrenalin flowing. After the high-octane excitement of war, even at secondhand in the press, peace was a humdrum business. The most law-abiding citizens felt, as time went by, that life would never be lived as fully again. As in any form of addiction, the symptoms of withdrawal were hard to endure and sometimes impossible to resist.

Bentley and the two Craig brothers needed no examples nor encouragement from the cinema screen, nor from fiction had they been able to read it. They and their fictional counterparts had been conditioned alike in childhood and youth by the world around them. They boy hero in *King of the Commandos* is at school on the south coast at the time of Dunkirk. Excitement reaches white-heat as two masters set out across the Channel in a leaky wherry to aid the evacuation, followed by two prefects who slip away in a dinghy. 'It was more than any normal healthy boy could stand,' and so the infant hero joins the armada of rescue on its way to France.

In all that was said of the criminal character of the Craig brothers, their first offences were usually overlooked. Christopher Craig, at fifteen, had been found with a revolver, sheltering under a boat in Brighton, on his journey to France. He was, it seemed, following a family tradition. In the middle of the war, Niven Craig and another schoolboy had robbed a Home Guard store to acquire weapons and had then set out in a rowing boat to cross the Channel and fight the Germans. The exhilaration of battle was everywhere and, as in *King of the Commandos*, 'it was more than any normal healthy boy could stand.' To judge from that, the creed of martial gallantry represented by Captain Johns and 'Gimlet' King had a formative influence to match anything offered by the dumb prose and unreal draughtsmanship of the American comics or the cinema-repertory melodrama of *My Death is a Mockery*.

CHAPTER 10

Despite a growing debate on crime and punishment, there was every sign that the authorities intended to move briskly to judgment in the case of Craig and Bentley. The case was set down for hearing at the Old Bailey on 4 December 1952, almost a month to the day from the death of Sidney Miles and a fortnight after Craig had been committed for trial by Croydon magistrates. The courts might be, as the *News Chronicle* put it on 18 December, 'jammed by a crime queue,' but that was not to prevent Craig and Bentley getting justice in short order.

The cast of the courtroom drama was soon chosen. As a tribute to the importance of the case, it was to be heard by the Lord Chief Justice of England, Lord Goddard. Seventy-five years old, he had been Lord Chief Justice since 1946. Rayner Goddard had been educated at Marlborough, Trinity College, Oxford, and Gray's Inn. He was called to the bar while Queen Victoria was still on the throne and had once been a Conservative parliamentary candidate. By 1952 the camera was no longer kind to him. In his wig and robes, the face seemed heavy and morose. He would, it suggested, be more inclined to vengeance than mercy. Indeed, he had a reputation for gallows humour and lewd stories in private that made his public righteousness still less palatable to his critics. One of his stories, quoted against him rather than about him, was of his amusement at an incident during Winchester Assizes. Goddard had just sentenced three men to death in the same case. As the judicial procession emerged from the court, a barrel-organ in the street was playing the *Eton Boating Song*. The tune had just reached the line, 'We'll all swing together,' which tickled his sense of humour. It was a story that he often repeated.

Goddard had been knighted by King George V on his

appointment as a high court judge in 1932. While he knelt before the sovereign, George V had one piece of advice for his new representative. 'Flog 'em!' said His Majesty. The royal advice was just what Goddard advocated twenty years later. Violence could only be cured by violence. Whether in holding such views Goddard was a political realist or a cantankerous old buffoon depended very much on the age and type of the person passing judgment. Other civilised nations managed the legal implementation of their criminal codes without resort to such punishments. But perhaps, in the case of the United States, they managed them much worse.

Throughout the summer of 1952, as the reports of violent crime grew more numerous and the alarm increased, there had been a national debate as to whether the birch or the cat o' nine tails might not curb the likes of Craig and Bentley. The argument was precipitated by Goddard at a Mansion House dinner on 3 July, when he suggested that flogging should not only be restored but its scope extended.

Eleven days before the death of PC Miles, Earl Howe had lamented to the House of Lords the abolition in 1948 of judicial flogging for crimes of violence. In his support, Lord Chief Justice Goddard had added that 'not only in country districts but in places as near here as even South Kensington many old people are terrified to answer a knock on the door at night.' The picture of a nation hiding at home after dark was just the one that Horace Walpole had described to Sir Thomas Mann two centuries before.

But it was Goddard's introduction of his political views on such matters in his courtroom remarks that caused most disquiet. He was apt to regret aloud that he could not have offenders before him flogged or punished in some such fashion, which led Michael Foot at the time to accuse him of acting the propagandist in court and so abusing his judicial power. It was a criticism that was heard even among members of the bar.

As usual, in the case of a man whose public personality was so evidently unsympathetic, there were not wanting voices to assure the world that he was gentle, charming, and affable in his private life. 'There were some of us who were privileged to see the other part of his life,' wrote Lord Denning, 'At home with his wife whom he adored, and three charming daughters; or on holiday by the sea in Dorset. Their welfare was his dearest concern. At the Bar-mess on Circuit or in the Lodgings. He was excellent company, telling his stories with zest; reciting "Albert and the Lion"; showing his knowledge of port and his taste for it. At a sip he could tell the very year of its vintage, and always correctly...' In the households of South London where the age of vintage port was not often put to the test, the private indulgences of Lord Goddard served only to make him seem more grotesque.

Though it was not out of the ordinary that the Lord Chief Justice should hear the case, the choice of Goddard did little to encourage any hope for Craig or Bentley. The prosecution was to be led by the Senior Treasury Counsel, Christmas Humphreys, QC, then at the peak of his career at the criminal bar and later to be a judge at the Old Bailey. Just over fifty years old, his performance in court was distinctive. He spoke in a flat and extremely rapid manner, so fast that the shorthand writers were sometimes hard put to it to keep up with him. In cross- examination his tone was apt to be haughty and hectoring.

Apart from his career at the bar, he was also a prominent Buddhist. But anyone who supposed that his religion led him to be a gentle and compassionate soul who shrank from sending a man to his death by virtue of forensic skill, misjudged Humphreys. He was a skilful advocate and unremitting in his zeal. In private, his interests were music and poetry, osteopathy and psychoanalysis. But they seemed to inculcate strength of purpose in his pursuit of justice, rather than weakness and speculation at the thought of what awaited the guilty.

The defence of Bentley was undertaken by Frank Cassels, an experienced criminal lawyer. However, the best hope for Bentley was that while he might be guilty of murder as a legal technicality, no one would sustain a conviction against him to the extreme of sending him to the gallows. Perhaps the principal difficulty was that Bentley denied saying, 'Let him have it, Chris,' as he denied making various other remarks. In this, he appeared to contradict corroborated police testimony. Three officers gave evidence that they had heard the words, 'Let him have it, Chris.' Mrs Tennent and others living in the neighbourhood had confirmed from their stories in the press that it was easy enough even for someone on the ground to hear what was being said on the warehouse roof at that time on that particular night.

The issue in court was simple. Whom would the jury believe? Bentley, whose courtroom performances rarely exceeded the level of, 'No, sir. Not me, sir,' or five police officers, each corroborating the evidence of the others? The headlines from Croydon, CORONER PRAISES FEARLESS POLICE ... WAVE OF CRIME 'A CHALLENGE' were scarcely a month old. Bentley was a self-confessed thief, a willing participant in the crime that led to Miles' death. How on earth could a jury be persuaded that he, and not the police witnesses, was telling the truth about anything?

Cassels' private opinion, expressed to John Parris, that Bentley 'ought to swing,' did not in itself make his efforts on behalf of his client less determined. At the lowest level of calculation, it would do his career more good to see Bentley acquitted or reprieved than to see him go to the gallows. But Cassels had an established reputation. The unknown legal figure in the trial was John Parris, a young Leeds barrister and Labour parliamentary candidate for Bradford North. Undaunted by his comparative lack of experience in the face of the Lord Chief Justice and Senior Treasury Counsel, Parris fought with conviction and tenacity for Craig. Moreover, he did so under two handicaps. The first was the very little time allowed him to gather evidence from his client and to prepare the case. The second was the impression that Craig gave the world. It was one of sulky indifference to charges against him, and a mood that appeared to differ little from downright unrepentance. He had expressed no remorse and no regret, except of the kind represented by such comments as, 'I wish I'd killed the fucking lot.'

The defence of Craig was in almost every respect a forlorn fight, though his life was not at stake. The best to be hoped for was that Parris could reduce the killing of PC Miles from murder to manslaughter. In other words, there could be no doubt that

Craig had fired the gun, but it might be suggested, as indeed Craig soon suggested, that he fired at random without any particular intention of hitting the police. Once again, however, Craig's own scornful words seemed to condemn him, no less than the unlucky chance of Sidney Miles being shot between the eyes. However inaccurate the sawn-off .455, the fatal wound suggested a careful and skilful aim.

Parris, of course, was in the curious situation of not even having heard of Craig when his clerk phoned him on a Sunday afternoon, two weeks after the murder of PC Miles, and told him that the brief for the defence had been accepted. Indeed, the situation was alarming as well as curious. He was required to appear for the defence at the Old Bailey, in a fortnight's time, in one of the most important murder trials for a century past. But Parris was already appearing at Leeds Assizes in the case of two men who were charged with receiving stolen gold from a Sheffield refinery. In the middle of this other case, on 2 December, the brief for the defence of Craig was delivered. It was two days before the trial was due to begin in London. As John Parris remarked, he could neither be at the Old Bailey nor even have a conference with his client by then.

He paid a flying visit to London, in the literal sense that he had to charter a private plane to get back to Leeds in time for his own brief at the assizes. In the office of the prosecuting solicitors he overheard Christmas Humphreys describing him as 'some young chap who hasn't been called long,' and suggesting that Parris had only got the brief because he was related to Croydon solicitors of the same name. The name of Craig's solicitors proved to be Nelson.

Counsel in the case met the Lord Chief Justice that morning, 2 December. Goddard was unwilling to delay the hearing, despite the difficulty of Parris being in London for it, let alone preparing the defence and interviewing his client. After what John Parris described as 'a good deal of argument,' Goddard agreed to postpone the start of the trial for five days. It would begin at the Old Bailey on Tuesday 9 December.

Parris's interviews with Craig during the intervening weekend produced the most vivid portrait of the defendant. 'The outstanding impression was one of femininity,' Parris later wrote, describing the dark brown eyes, smooth skin and soft bow-shaped lips. The voice and manner were 'diffident and gentle.' Parris guessed, perhaps most shrewdly of all, that Craig's conduct had nothing to do with films, comics and the like. It was an attempt to establish his masculinity against the more feminine impression that he conveyed.

Ironically, Craig was in that respect united with those who were loudest and shrillest in their condemnation of the new generation of teenagers. They and he, in varying ways, believed that arms and combat made the man. In Craig's view it was the experience of the adolescent street-fighter that was to do the trick, in the other opinion it was conscription for military service. Born ten years earlier, he might have fulfilled himself in 1939–1945, as his father had done in 1914–1918.

At Brixton prison, Parris found his client wearing clothes fit for an 'American gangster,' a suede jacket, blue trousers, and suede shoes. He told Craig to see that his parents bought him something more appropriate for his court appearance. When the trial opened he was more quietly dressed in a sports-jacket and flannels.

But the public already knew too many details of Craig for a change of clothes to do him much good. The preliminary hearings before Croydon magistrates had been reported in the national press under such headlines as those of 18 November, POLICE TELL OF GUN FIGHT WITH CRAIG. And for good measure there had been the first news of the incident in the brisk prose of papers like the *Daily Mail*, which wrote of Chicago-style gangsters machine-gunning the police over the rooftops of South London. All that was fresh and renewed in the public memory.

In addition to that, there was already something of a three-ring circus now that the press had made substantial investments in the case. The Craig family and their story had been bought by the *Sunday Pictorial*, determined not to have its scoop spoilt by letting other journalists get at them. High windows round the Old Bailey had been booked and Sandy Powell was ready with his camera for an ascent by crane. There was still less interest in Bentley. He may not have been quite the 'drooling dim-witted Bentley' that one of his campaigners, R. T. Paget, claimed. All the same, it was Craig who now represented value for the journalists' money.

Then, two days before the trial was due to begin, the case was wiped from the pages of the newspapers and the minds of their readers by a story of sudden and dramatic relevance. The greatest smog of all time descended on London and the Home Counties. It was no ordinary mist or fog but a sulphurous yellow-grey smoke, thick enough to make one side of a street invisible from the other. There was no daylight and no clean air to breathe. The elderly and those whose lungs were weak for any reason died in their hundreds. Hospitals were taken off guard by the extent of the emergency. Traffic was almost at a standstill in the centre of the capital, the London streets strangely quiet and dead. Trains ran slowly on the Sunday, when they ran at all. Ferry passengers were fogbound all night in the Channel. Life in the city slowed down to a blind crawl. This suited the city's robbers. STREET ATTACKS IN FOG, ran the headlines, HOUSEBREAKERS ACTIVE. Others were less active. The smog brought with it a razor-edged winter chill. The people of London, caught by this sharp and sudden affliction, found that they had more immediate concerns than the fate of Bentley or Craig.

John Parris 'battled', as he put it, to reach Brixton prison through the poisonous and freezing yellow vapour. He had a second interview with his client. When that had been done, he was left with less than forty-eight hours to prepare his case.

The unseasonable weather did not deter the Lord Chief Justice. On the preceding Thursday he had caused something of a stir over his remarks from the bench. He had been dealing with a pair of teenage brothers who had robbed two other boys while threatening them with an air-gun and an air-pistol. 'Nowadays,' Goddard growled at the court, 'the cane is never used at school. It would have done them good if they had had a good larruping. What they want is to have someone who would give them a thundering good beating... I suppose they were brought up to be treated like little darlings, and tucked up in bed at night.'

To believe that the cane was never used at school in 1952

suggested that Goddard was less in touch with the truths of English life than he wished to appear. Boys, and indeed girls, were still being caned at school. But as Dr Wertheim reassured his readers, if they developed a taste for sado-masochism in any form the cause might be directly traced to the reading of crime comics. In the case of the two boys, it later transpired that they came from a home where their father beat them every night. It was brutality and not pampering that had made them what they were. All the same, five days before the case of Craig and Bentley began, the Lord Chief Justice appeared to be telling the public what it wanted to hear.

He sent the elder boy to Borstal and the younger to an approved school.

'Nowadays, courts cannot deal with you boys as you ought to be dealt with,' he grumbled at them, 'Magistrates can do nothing to you, and this court can hardly do anything to you.'

In the freezing fog of Monday morning, the day before the trial of Craig and Bentley, Goddard returned to the Old Bailey. Two fifteen-year-old boys who had held up another with a knife and a stick were appealing against sentences of detention imposed on them by a lower court. Goddard dismissed the appeal and mentioned the case of the other two boys on the previous Thursday, regretting that he had not been able to deal more severely with them. As for the present appellants, his main concern was that they would not be treated harshly enough during their sentences. They would be sent to an approved schoool, 'which is a delightful place – possibly too delightful. It is to be hoped that they will get some discipline there. Boys must understand that if they do things like this, something unpleasant will follow. Very often, they go home from these approved schools and tell their friends to do something, because they will get sent there and it is so nice.' The press caught this next morning with the headline LORD GODDARD ON APPROVED SCHOOLS – DELIGHTFUL.

The hysterias and phobias of one age are usually sinister or comic to its ungrateful successors. Had Rayner Goddard implemented in 1987 the punishment he judged appropriate in

December 1952, the nation might have been diverted by the sight of the Lord Chief Justice spending a few years behind bars for child abuse. By the same token, the fact that a little girl should ask a man exercising his dog if she could go for a walk with him, would have seemed engaging or perhaps affecting at any period not beset by the child abuse phobia of 1987, when the Childwatch organisation thought the incident worthy of mention in *The Times* on 26 August to indicate the desperate perils facing the nation's young. That such preoccupations seem bizarre by hindsight is one more indication of the intensity with which they are felt.

Lord Goddard spoke for a majority of the nation on that Monday morning, ill-informed and vindictive though he might seem. By the next day the visible fog had begun to clear a little from the London streets. Tickets were issued to important people wanting to watch the trial of the two teenage murderers. Humbler folk queued patiently and for the most part vainly for the few seats in the public gallery. Crowds packed the streets round the Old Bailey to see the arrival of the prison vans from Brixton, perhaps even to catch a glimpse of the accused. A Rolls Royce drew up, containing the other members of the Craig family and their bodyguard from the *Sunday Pictorial*. They posed briefly while the cameras of colleagues and rivals clicked and popped and flashed. Harry Proctor, the *Sunday Pictorial* journalist who was responsible for minding the family and ensuring their comments were not poached, later described his guardianship of them as being run like a military operation. There was to be one exclusive denied to the *Pictorial*, however. Mr Craig was to give evidence for the prosecution. Whatever he said under questioning in the witness-box would be public property.

John Parris, arriving on foot from the bus stop at the bottom of the street, was in time to see the Craig family's appearance. Mr Craig was expressionless, his wife had been crying, their daughter Lucy was beautiful enough to be breathtaking. No one could deny that the *Pictorial* was doing them proud. Derek Bentley's parents arrived almost unnoticed by public transport from Norbury. To them, the ways of the Central Criminal Court and the intricacies of legal argument were as bewildering and intimidating as the laws of molecular biology or quantum physics.

As if it were Wimbledon or a West End first-night, some of the privileged ticket-holders had sold out to the touts. Tickets for the show were reputed to be changing hands at £30 each, about two or three weeks' salary for most of those standing in the gallery queue. At length the door closed and the queue stopped moving. It was half-past ten. Inside No. 2 Court of the Old Bailey, the curtain was about to go up.

CHAPTER 11

At 10.30, the Lord Chief Justice took his place on the bench and those who were upstanding in court sat down again. Craig had graduated from stretcher to wheelchair and was by now able to stand with the aid of sticks. He appeared in the dock next to Bentley. They were formally charged with murdering Sidney George Miles and each pleaded not guilty. Goddard made his only concession of the case. He stared at the two accused youths in the dock for a long moment and then said, 'Craig may sit down.'

While the jury was being sworn in, John Parris objected to two women jurors. The reasons, which he gave later, were familiar enough. He was unknown at the Old Bailey, let alone to the jury, and it was important to create some kind of impression upon them as early as possible in the case. It might even serve to put prosecuting counsel off his stroke just before the opening speech for the Crown. In addition, Parris thought women would be more likely than men to convict in a case of violent crime. The horror of it and the prospect that they might themselves have been victims would lead them to this.

Christmas Humphreys, opening the case for the Crown, led the jury patiently through the events of Sunday evening, 2 November, in Tamworth Road. He conceded that the night had been dark. Evidence might be affected by that. But he was emphatic that Bentley had said, 'Let him have it, Chris,' while Fairfax was holding him. 'The immediate reply to that comment by Bentley,' Humphreys added, 'was a loud report, and Fairfax was hit on the shoulder with what turned out to be a bullet from the gun which Craig held.'

That was the crux of the prosecution case. Bentley knew that Craig was carrying a gun. While detained by Fairfax, he urged

Craig to use the gun. The gun was used without hesitation. On the first occasion it wounded Fairfax. Next time it killed Miles. That a gap of quarter of an hour separated the two shots which found their targets did not matter. That Bentley was under arrest before Miles was killed did not matter either. In Humphreys' submission, Bentley had been a partner with Craig in initiating the gun battle. Bentley could no more avoid responsibility than if he had rolled a boulder from the top of a hill and had been arrested before it killed a man at the bottom.

'Let him have it, Chris,' were the words of which a noose was made. Guiding the jury by means of copies of the scale-drawing with which they had been provided, Humphreys continued his exposition. When Miles was shot, it was by a bullet 'straight between the eyes.' The phrase hardly suggested that Craig was firing at random. And then there was the scornful defiance as Miles fell dead. 'I am Craig. You've just given my brother twelve years. Come on, you coppers. I'm only sixteen.'

Craig sat through Humphreys' account, apparently indifferent to its effect on the jury. Bentley was now in a strange world of legal subtlety that he could not begin to comprehend. Humphreys described how Bentley, as Fairfax and McDonald led him to the stairs, shouted, 'Look out, Chris, they're taking me down.' Was it, Humphreys suggested, 'A further invitation? Cry for help?' Even though Bentley was under arrest, was he not still inciting Craig to shoot the police officers and set him free? A more articulate defendant might have made short work of that suggestion, the commonsense deduction being that Bentley was telling Craig not to fire for fear of being hit himself. But articulation and argument were not Bentley's forte.

Humphreys described the conclusion of the gun fight, 'if such it was,' and read out most of Bentley's statement to the police. He reminded the jurors that once both accused were under arrest, statements made by either could not be used as evidence against the other. That scarcely mattered. Bentley's life was the only one at stake. But there followed a recital of Craig's remarks in hospital which served to blacken the criminal purpose of them both.

As if anticipating that Craig's defence might be a plea of

manslaughter, Humphreys pointed out that as many bullets and cartridge cases as could be found were later collected from the scene. By no means all of them were accounted for. However, Craig had fired at least nine shots from a gun that would hold six. Humphreys made the significance plain for the jurors.

'The importance of that fact is this, that the revolver only holds six, and that means that at some period or periods during the fight Craig, who alone had the ammunition, was reloading. The importance of that to you is to show a deliberate purpose in his mind, as distinct from a foolish boy who happened to have a loaded gun and in fear or losing his head, whatever it may be, pulls the trigger.'

So much for manslaughter. In any case, there were to be no 'boys' in Humphreys' case. He had referred early on in his opening speech to Craig and Bentley as 'the men' who confronted the police on the roof of Barlow and Parker's warehouse.

'The case for the Crown is this and nothing less,' Humphreys concluded, 'that Craig deliberately murdered PC Miles and, as I have said, thereafter gloried in the murder and only regretted he had not shot more. Bentley incited Craig to begin the shooting, and although he was technically under arrest at the time of the actual murder of PC Miles, was nevertheless still mentally supporting Craig in all that Craig continued to do. And in English law, and you may think in common sense, was in every sense party to that murder.'

As Humphreys sat down and his junior, J. T. Bass, began the examination of the prosecution witnesses, several journalists slipped from the court to phone their stories. The Lunch Edition of the *Evening Standard* was on the street with it first. Its readers were not to be disappointed. CRAIG TRIAL OPENS, ran the banner headline across the front page, 'HE GLORIED IN THE MURDER.' And that, once again, was what the public wanted to hear.

But the morning was not yet over at the Old Bailey. Bass and Humphreys began to call the witnesses for the prosecution. The first evidence was pure formality and the attention of the spectators wandered to the two ill-matched figures in the dock

and to Lord Goddard in his place above the court, his features set
in the familiar lines of stony disapproval. PC Beard, the police
draughtsman from 'Z' Division, identified the plan of the
warehouse he had drawn as being accurate. Chief Inspector Law
of Scotland Yard's Photographic Department did the same for his
photographs of the scene. Though undramatic and unchallenged,
the evidence was crucial to Humphreys' case. He was leading the
jury through the facts by reference to plan and photographs. Had
they not been 'proved,' his entire case might have been challenged
when it was too late to repair the damage.

A few minutes later, attention returned to the witness-box.
The prosecution now called Niven Matthews Craig, the father of
the accused youth. This was done in order to introduce the birth
certificate of Christopher Craig, showing him to have been born
on 19 May 1936. He might be too young to hang, but it was to be
clear that he had reached the age of criminal responsibility.
J. T. Bass asked the father no other questions initially except his
name, address, and occupation. But by calling Mr Craig, he laid
him open to cross-examination by the defence. Frank Cassels, for
Bentley, asked no questions. John Parris took the opportunity to
show a side of Christopher Craig's personality that the public had
so far been denied. In doing this he naturally found Mr Craig a
most co-operative subject.

When the witness answered questions about himself as a citizen
and a father, every word seemed borne out by his appearance and
manner. He was a smart, neatly-moustached man, dark haired and
solidly built, who looked every inch the ex-officer. He was a
trusted senior official in a London bank. The jury appeared to be
impressed. As a parent, Mr Craig had done his best for his son's
education, despite the 'word blindness' or dyslexia from which the
boy suffered. Had not Mr Craig tried, unavailingly, 'night after
night' to teach him to read?

'Oh, I did indeed, sir.'

Then came the revelation that, apart from the Bible, Craig's
sole literary inspiration came from comics and the children's books
of Enid Blyton. The jury's interest grew. This was not at all the
sort of boy who had been previously described to them. John

Parris turned to Mr Craig's past record and demonstrated that he served with distinction as an officer in 1914–1918. So much for the image of a loutish son and indifferent parents. Mr Craig confessed that he himself had one criminal conviction. During the Second World War, while serving in the Home Guard, he had a revolver and a licence for it. Someone gave him a second gun that was not in working order. He omitted to get a separate licence for that and was fined. It was hardly enough to damage the reputation that John Parris was building for him.

Goddard intervened, as he frequently did during Parris's examinations, demanding to know the point of such questions and insisting that Parris must 'keep within some bounds.' As the cross-examination continued, Mr Craig described how he had taught his sons to shoot on a rifle range. Though Christopher remained a poor shot, the boy's ambition had been to become a gunsmith.

Most important of all, Mr Craig denied that his son was ever violent in the past. He was 'quite the opposite... Very gentle.'

It was too late by now for the evening papers, who had got their story in any case. But next morning the headlines presented a riddle of character. CHRISTOPHER CRAIG: GENTLE BOY OR RUTHLESS GUNMAN? 'The boy who used to get other people to read to him from the children's books of Enid Blyton sat yesterday in the dock at the Old Bailey, charged with the murder of a policeman.'

But the court had not yet done with Mr Craig. When John Parris sat down, Christmas Humphreys got up to dispel something of the respectability which had gathered round his witness. Unfortunately, he seemed to misread, or perhaps misunderstand, his instructions when he asked whether Mr Craig's conviction for possessing a gun without a licence was not in March 1952, soon after his son's? Recently convicted for a firearms offence, Mr Craig might not have seemed so impressive to the jury. Like father, like son, it was suggested. However, the date of the conviction was 1942, not 1952, and Mr Craig put him right about that.

Goddard intervened, asking for details of Christopher Craig's attempt to run off to Brighton and catch a boat to France. It was, the Lord Chief Justice supposed, 'a sort of frolic on his own.' Mr Craig agreed. He admitted that he did not know of the 124 rounds of ammunition and twenty-five air-gun pellets hidden by his son under the attic floor, which was not surprising. And, with that, his evidence was at an end.

Mrs Ware, whose husband had raised the alarm by phoning the police on that Sunday night, gave evidence that she had seen two men on the opposite pavement, one of them shorter than the other. She saw the shorter one climb over the side gate of the warehouse, followed by the taller one. She did not identify them as Craig and Bentley, though it was assumed that they must have been the pair in the dock.

The rest of the morning was taken up by the most important of the prosecution witnesses, Frederick Fairfax, Detective Constable at the time of the murder but Detective Sergeant by the start of the trial.

Christmas Humphreys took Fairfax through the familiar chronology of the gun battle on the warehouse roof. Fairfax insisted that when he grabbed hold of Bentley, the prisoner presently broke away and shouted, 'Let him have it, Chris!'

Then at once came the flash, the loud report, something striking Fairfax's right shoulder so that he spun round and fell to the ground. All of that was plain enough. But then Humphreys, as if trying to clarify for the jury the darkness and confusion of the rooftop struggle, asked Fairfax, 'To get it clear: as a result of your being shot and knocked down, Bentley had got out of your grasp?'

'Yes,' Fairfax said.

Question and answer compounded the confusion. If it was not until the shot had been fired that Fairfax lost his hold on Bentley, that cast doubt on the whole story of Bentley inciting Craig to use his gun. He would hardly have referred to the gun by shouting, 'Let him have it, Chris!' while in the policeman's grip, when the bullet was as likely to hit him as Fairfax. Up to this time, the police evidence had been unequivocal in placing the three figures on the roof in positions to substantiate Bentley's guilt. Fairfax now contradicted that version of events.

In summary, the previous order of events had been:

1. Bentley broke away from Fairfax's hold.
2. Bentley shouted, 'Let him have it, Chris!'
3. Craig shot Fairfax in the shoulder from a range of about six feet.

The new order was significantly different.

1. Bentley was in Fairfax's grip.
2. Craig shot Fairfax in the shoulder.
3. Fairfax fell and only then lost hold of Bentley.

These inconsistencies made little difference to Craig's act of murder. But they directly affected the fate of Bentley who was the only one on trial for his life. In the second order of events, if Bentley had shouted, 'Let him have it, Chris,' while still being held by Fairfax, it was not unreasonable to assume that he thought Craig would let Fairfax 'have it' with knuckleduster or fist. Unlike a shot from a gun, that would not have endangered Bentley himself while Fairfax was holding him.

Fairfax went on to recall the second damning comment by Bentley, that Craig had 'a .45 Colt and plenty of bloody ammunition too.' It was further apparent evidence that he had known Craig would carry a gun that night. Humphreys took his witness through the rest of the story without any further variation on the case as the prosecution had presented it.

John Parris was the first of the two defence counsel to cross-examine Fairfax. His strategy was still to show that Craig had been guilty of manslaughter rather than murder. But he first questioned Fairfax as to the exact number of shots that had been fired. So far, Fairfax had mentioned only three before Miles was killed. There were the two fired at him and the one that had hit Miles. Now he added 'somewhere like six or seven other shots' between those fired at him and the one that hit Miles.

'Did you see where they came from?'

'No,' Fairfax said.

Under the circumstances, it seemed that they must have been fired by Craig. There were no armed policemen at the warehouse by then. Only much later did Parris reveal a further possibility, which it would have been impossible to demonstrate during the trial. From what he had learnt, presumably through Craig, there were not two youths on the warehouse roof that night but three.

The cross-examination continued, Parris endeavouring to show that Fairfax was standing at a considerable distance when the bullet hit his shoulder and, by inference, that Craig was firing to scare him away and not to hit him. Fairfax denied this, adding that 'at the time of the first shot, he (Bentley) was not in my grasp; he had already broken away from me.' This was in contradiction to what Fairfax had said when Humphreys tried 'to get it clear.'

It was not surprising that Fairfax should have found it difficult to be precise in certain details. Events had moved quickly on the warehouse roof. As Parris suggested, it was dark and confusing. Fairfax had, without question, behaved gallantly in tackling the two suspects, even when he knew Craig was armed. But precise recollection cannot have been helped by his 'certain degree of shock' which Dr Jazwon observed at Croydon General Hospital. Far from diminishing Fairfax's bravery, it bore witness to the ordeal of unequal combat on the asphalt roof. By the time he reached hospital, he had been shot himself, he had seen a close colleague shot between the eyes, and watched a boy of sixteen attempt a suicide dive from the roof. A man who suffered no shock at such events occurring in the course of half an hour would have been scarcely human.

Having established that Craig, as Fairfax remembered, fired 'about ten shots,' John Parris sat down and left the witness to be cross-examined further by Frank Cassels on behalf of Bentley. Cassels came presently to the contradiction in Fairfax's answers to Christmas Humphreys.

'You see, I do not want to take advantage of any slip. But you did agree with my learned friend, Mr Humphreys, that Bentley broke away after the shot was fired.'

'If I did,' Fairfax replied, 'I have made a mistake, because Bentley actually broke away from me before the shot was fired.'

Goddard was having no more nonsense about inconsistencies. So far he had interrupted the witnesses only to clarify various points. Now he announced what it was that Fairfax had said.

Ignoring the second reply, Goddard insisted that it was the first answer that counted. Bentley had broken away, shouted to Craig, and then the shot was fired.

'I quite agree, my lord,' said Cassels patiently, going on to remind Goddard of the second and inconsistent reply from Fairfax to Humphreys. Yet there was nothing for it but to accept a genuine mistake by the witness and find another way forward. So Cassels suggested that Bentley had never shouted, 'Let him have it, Chris!' Fairfax insisted that he did. Cassels then suggested that it was Craig, not Bentley, who made the remark about the '.45 Colt.' Again Fairfax insisted that it was Bentley who had spoken. Craig might have said something about it as well but, if so, Fairfax had not heard him.

Goddard intervened, making the point that the word used was 'he' and not 'I.' In that case, the words must have been spoken by Bentley.

It was as far as Cassels could get in that direction. He tried to show that Bentley was a willing prisoner once the first shot had been fired. But while Fairfax dragged Bentley back to the head of the staircase, he recalled that his prisoner was still resisting. Fairfax, by his own account, was using him as a shield against Craig's bullets, so perhaps Bentley's struggles were not wholly surprising. Once in the shelter of the well-head, Bentley had resisted no longer. He had been free to escape when Fairfax needed both hands to help McDonald up but had made no attempt to get away.

Finally, Cassels questioned Fairfax as to when he had made notes of the events on the roof. But Fairfax had been hit on the right shoulder and understandably he had made no notes in the aftermath of the shooting. His version of the fight came in a statement which he dictated in hospital between 1am and 2am the next morning. As if hinting that several of the officers on the roof had agreed to allege Bentley's, 'Let him have it, Chris!' Cassels asked, 'Had a number of police officers been to see you in hospital before you dictated that statement?'

Only Detective-Sergeant Shepherd and Chief Inspector Smith, Fairfax said. It was not beyond possibility that 'Let him have it,

Chris!' was concocted by the police within a few hours of the shooting. The choice of whether to believe the police witnesses or Bentley in that matter remained with the jury.

When Fairfax had finished his evidence, Goddard adjourned for lunch. As Craig was being taken down the steps of the dock, he made one final remark about Fairfax for the benefit of the warder escorting him.

'I ought to have killed that fucker as well!'

John Parris was merely grateful that the comment was not overheard by the jury.

On Tuesday afternoon, the court was occupied in hearing evidence from more prosecution witnesses. Three police officers who had been on the warehouse roof with Fairfax and one who had seen Craig land in the yard behind the building were called. So were two more who had been in the police car returning to the station when Bentley made his alleged remark about knowing Craig had a gun but not thinking he would use it.

PC McDonald, who reached the roof second with Fairfax's assistance, testified that while he was climbing the drainpipe he had heard someone shout, 'Let him have it, Chris!' It was not a voice he knew at the time.

'Have you heard the same voice since?' asked Mr J. T. Bass, Humphreys' junior.

'I could not say for certain.'

At the very least this was an interesting answer. McDonald had certainly heard Bentley's voice since. Indeed, he now gave evidence as to what Bentley had said while in his custody on the roof. But the voice which shouted the all-important words was beyond identification. David Yallop was later to suggest that since the officer's name was James Christie McDonald, the encouragement to 'let him have it' – 'him' presumably being the gunman – may have been directed at McDonald by another policeman. But other evidence in the case makes clear that McDonald was familiarly known as 'Mac' and not by his middle name.

McDonald also recalled Bentley's words, 'I told the silly bugger not to use it,' again suggesting that he knew of Craig's gun. And

McDonald had seen Craig firing at PC Harrison who was moving along an adjoining roof. He had been careful and correct in his evidence, never referring to Craig by name, since it had been impossible to identify him then in the dark, but talking of 'the man on the roof.'

The Lord Chief Justice had had enough of this.

'Of course, you know now that the man on the roof was Craig?'

McDonald did know it now.

'Well,' Goddard said, 'we can call him Craig instead of "the man on the roof." '

In cross-examination, John Parris tried to establish that Craig's shots had been fired at random and not aimed at any particular officer. It was once more the argument of manslaughter rather than murder. He suggested to McDonald that Craig fired in general 'over the rooftop.'

'I would not know exactly where the shots went,' McDonald said, 'but they were pointing towards the right of the building where PC Harrison was.'

Parris tried to press the point, but Lord Goddard was back again.

'He says they were aimed at Harrison, but he does not know where they went. Is that what you mean?'

'Yes,' said PC McDonald.

'Is this the position,' Parris asked, 'you saw a shot fired in his direction, but you could not say it was aimed at Harrison?'

'That is correct,' McDonald said, going back on what he said he meant when the Lord Chief Justice intervened. Goddard interrupted to put him right again.

'You saw him point the gun at Harrison?'

'I saw him point the gun at Harrison and he fired the shot.'

Parris, undaunted at his baptism by judicial fire in the Central Criminal Court, pressed McDonald again, this time on the number of shots that had been fired. Goddard was not prepared to tolerate it, though he had allowed Christmas Humphreys to put the number at about nine, which required Craig to show his murderous intent by reloading. Fairfax had suggested ten without being reprimanded. But the Lord Chief Justice now took a different view of this question from the defence.

'I wonder,' Goddard said, 'how anybody could be expected to be accurate on a matter like this, on a night like this when these men are being fired at, in fear of their lives, and now they are being asked weeks afterwards to count how many shots were fired.'

In a case which meant life or death for nineteen-year-old Derek Bentley, the greatest possible accuracy seemed desirable. And, indeed, McDonald had given the total number of shots as ten or eleven. Since Fairfax had put it at ten, what was now sought seemed more like confirmation than accuracy.

When Frank Cassels cross-examined McDonald, the witness insisted that he had heard the words, 'Let him have it, Chris,' but that he could not identify the voice. Goddard was not prepared to tolerate unnecessary doubt. He intervened again. Had McDonald heard the word 'Chris'? He had.

'So far as you know, there were three people on the roof?'
'Yes.'
'There was Sergeant Fairfax and the two men?'
'Yes.'
'And you heard: "Let him have it, Chris." Is that right?'
'That is right, my lord.'

Goddard let it go at that. McDonald might not have been able to identify the voice but the Lord Chief Justice had done it for him.

McDonald's evidence, though nowhere favourable to the accused, differed in significant details from that of Fairfax. Fairfax recalled Bentley saying 'He's got a .45 Colt.' McDonald remembered 'It's a .45 Colt.' Though he attributed the remark to Bentley, it was at least grammatically possible that it had been made by Craig. Had there been collusion between the police witnesses, such discrepancies might well have been ironed out. McDonald gave the impression of being a conscientious witness. He was all the more impressive because while confirming that Fairfax and not Bentley had told the truth as to what was said, he differed from Fairfax over certain details.

In reply to Frank Cassels, he revealed that while on the drainpipe he had heard the words 'Let him have it, Chris,' and the first shot. But he had not heard the shot fired as an immediate response, which was how Fairfax described it. There had been an interval between the words and the shot, a time long enough for him to climb down the length of the drainpipe. It had been a pause of minutes rather than seconds.

At the very least this cast some doubt on whether the words were the immediate cause of the shot. 'Minutes' made it seem like a long time. But Goddard was not prepared to put up with this either. Addressing the court at large, he assured them, 'People can always say minutes when they mean seconds in these cases.'

Four times in the course of McDonald's evidence, Goddard had told him what it was that he really meant. The final comment about minutes and seconds, if taken at all literally, would have made nonsense of almost all the evidence in the case. That it had been PC McDonald and not Lord Goddard who was actually there, climbing up and then down the drainpipe, seemed to count for nothing.

PC Norman Harrison followed McDonald in the witness-box. He had been overlooking the flat roof from another roof before Fairfax appeared. He confirmed Fairfax's account of two shots being fired immediately after Bentley broke away and shouted at Craig to let him have it. But, curiously, he had not seen Craig or Bentley when Fairfax approached them, nor had he heard Craig's shout, 'If you want us, fucking well come and get us!' When John Parris suggested to him that his recollection did not tally with that of McDonald and asked him if McDonald's placing of Craig at another point on the roof was right or wrong, Goddard interposed again.

'You need not tell us whether one man is right or wrong. You tell us what you remember and what you saw.'

The remainder of the evidence from police officers present at Tamworth Road was less vigorously challenged. Frank Cassels, however, contested the claim that Bentley, while in the police car, had said, 'I knew he had a gun, but I didn't think he'd use it. He's done one of your blokes in.'

Both Sergeant Roberts and PC Stephens maintained that Bentley had used the words and that he had done so spontaneously. They denied that any questions had been asked him about the gun or about the identity of the gunman on the roof. It seemed strange that no one had done so, that there was not more curiosity about who was firing on the police but the question might have been put by police officers who did not give evidence or make statements.

The medical evidence which followed was characterised by a number of interventions from Goddard, hostile to the defence counsel and particularly to John Parris. The spent bullet which had grazed Fairfax's shoulder was found lodged in the back of his braces. Parris, attempting to show that Craig had merely fired at the ground to frighten Fairfax away, asked Dr Jazwon, the casualty officer, whether the evidence of his examination was consistent with a bullet ricochetting up from the ground, searing the shoulder, and then going down behind the back.

'The doctor is here to give medical evidence,' Goddard said sharply, 'not to speculate on the flight of bullets.'

'I was asking whether what he found, the wound, is consistent with that theory.'

'That is a matter you can address the jury on. It is not a matter for the doctor.'

Anyone who hoped that Goddard might have been mellowed by a good lunch was soon to be disillusioned. He grumbled at the decision to bring Dr Jazwon to court at all. His evidence 'could have been perfectly well read.'

Dr Haler the pathologist gave evidence that Miles had been shot through the head and that the wounds at entry and exit were typical of 'a bullet of large calibre.' He was not cross-examined on this.

The point of contention, in medical terms, was over the treatment of Christopher Craig in Croydon General Hospital. His sardonic and scornful comments in the week following the shooting were part of the prosecution evidence. They hardly suggested a frightened youth who had fired at random and was guilty of no more than manslaughter. Later in the afternoon, various police officers who had kept watch by his hospital bed were called to give evidence of his outbursts. Each time that a sentence like, 'All you bastards should be dead,' or, 'I shot him in the head and he went down like a ton of bricks' was read out, the avenue of escape for the defendants seemed to shrivel to invisibility.

John Parris tried to show that Craig was either distraught with pain from his injuries or else under the influence of drugs when he made such remarks. He cross-examined Dr Gordon Hatfield, medical officer at Croydon General Hospital, on the use of pentathol which Craig was given as an anaesthetic and pethadrine which he was given as a pain-killer. Pentathol had acquired the reputation of a 'truth-drug', but its use in a large quantity for an operation would not have had that result and its effect would have worn off very quickly. Pethadrine might give a feeling of elation but that was not usual. Parris was obliged to fall back on the suggestion that patients varied in their response to drugs and that Craig's reaction might not have been typical. But in the end there was no evidence, one way or the other, on this.

Detective-Sergeant Shepherd gave evidence of the search carried out at the home of the Craig family and the taking of Bentley's statement. Frank Cassels challenged the method by which the statement was obtained, suggesting that it was prompted by questions and not given voluntarily. Shepherd denied this.

By the time that the first day of the trial was over, the evidence for the prosecution was almost complete. Whatever the feeling of the spectators about Lord Goddard, he had kept proceedings moving at a fair speed. The only two prosecution witnesses left for Wednesday morning were Chief Inspector Smith and the Director of the Metropolitan Police Laboratory who would give ballistics evidence.

But it was not the police witnesses and the experts for whom the enthusiasts queued all night outside the door of the public gallery, while the freezing mist gathered again along Old Bailey and about Holborn Viaduct. On the second day the two stars of the drama were to appear, the only witnesses for the defence:

Christopher Craig and Derek Bentley. The enthusiasts shivered in the dark and quiet street, counting the quarters that sounded from St Paul's on the hill above them. The spectacle would be well worth waiting for.

CHAPTER 12

John Leslie Smith, the Chief Inspector in charge of the investigation after Miles had been killed, was the first witness on Wednesday morning. His principal contribution was in giving evidence of the gun Craig had used and the number of bullets fired. When Smith was handed the revolver on 2 November, four of the chambers had been fired and there were bullets in the other two which had been struck by the hammer but failed to fire. In addition to the four spent cartridge cases in the revolver, three more had been found on the warehouse roof near the lift shaft, from which Craig was firing.

As John Parris pointed out in cross-examination, Smith's evidence accounted for seven bullets having been fired in all and the gun twice having failed to go off. In addition, the possibility existed that the police search had failed to find other cartridge cases. The maximum number of shots recalled by police witnesses was ten or eleven and that seemed not unreasonable. If Craig started with all six chambers loaded and fired these, reloaded, and then managed to fire four of the second six, that would give ten shots in all. There was nothing unusual in the police failing to find three of the cartridge cases, given the nature of the area to be searched.

Frank Cassels, in cross-examination, pressed Chief Inspector Smith on the statement Bentley had made six hours after the murder. Did the Chief Inspector agree that Bentley was below average intelligence?

'Oh, yes,' Smith said.

'Well below it?'

'Below it, sir. I cannot say well below it.'

'So far as you can ascertain, is he capable of reading and writing anything else but his own name?'

'He can. His schoolmaster said that he could, but with difficulty.'

For the first time, the jury began to get an inkling of Bentley's stunted mentality. But when Cassels suggested that Smith and Shepherd had questioned Bentley and formed a statement from his answers, Smith denied it. The only question put to him had been to establish that the events happened on 2 November 1952, since Bentley was at a loss to think of what that day's date might be.

Chief Inspector Smith made one concession, however. Cassels put a rephrased question.

'What I am suggesting is this, that with this below-average-intelligence young man, you had to jog his memory a bit in order to get the statement from him.'

'Well,' said Smith at length, 'if you can call repeating, perhaps, what he had said before "jogging his memory," yes.'

'Detective-Sergeant Shepherd repeated what he was writing down, did he?'

'He would read what had been written before, and occasionally Bentley would ask, "What have I said before?" He was very deliberate about this and thought quite a long time before he spoke and obviously occasionally he got a little out of context.'

But Smith insisted that Bentley's comment, 'I didn't know he was going to use the gun,' was spontaneous and not in reply to being asked a question about the gun.

The last witness of all was Lewis Charles Nickolls, Director of the Metropolitan Police Laboratory. He confirmed that he had examined the cartridge cases and two spent bullets, all .45 calibre, as well as the Eley .455 revolver, which he agreed was 'in good working order,' despite the shortening of its barrel.

The ammunition that Craig was using was slightly small for the Eley revolver. Nickolls described the effect of this as being that the bullet would leave the gun at an angle, instead of with a proper trajectory, and it would lose some of its power by the escape of gases at its sides. Indeed, the type of ammunition Craig was using would not have fitted the gun at all. The base of each round was too thick. But Nickolls found that Craig had filed the base of each 'to secure the proper firing of the weapon.'

John Parris began his cross-examination by suggesting that one of the two spent bullets found, lying by the staircase well-head, had been the bullet that killed Sidney Miles. But Nickolls had found no blood upon it and thought it was probably not the one. In that case, it seemed the fatal bullet had never been found. Dr Haler, who performed the post-mortem on Miles, had given evidence that it was large calibre, presumably a .45 or just possibly a .38. But so long as the bullet could not be found, an important item was missing from the evidence of the case. One cartridge case of .32 ammunition had been found on the roof. This was presumably from the .32 automatic with which Fairfax had been issued.

Parris next suggested that by shortening the barrel of the revolver and removing the sight, as well as by removing such a length of the rifling, Craig had made the weapon 'wholly inaccurate.'

'It becomes less accurate,' Nickolls answered precisely.

'Well, how inaccurate would you say that would make it?'

'I should say that this weapon, certainly in the hands of a person unaccustomed to firing it, was quite an inaccurate weapon.'

Parris was still building up the defence of manslaughter, showing that Craig could not possibly have aimed at Fairfax or Miles with any hope of hitting them. He tried to pin the witness down, in terms that the jury would understand at once.

'May I put it to you that it would be inaccurate to the degree of six feet at a range of thirty-nine feet?'

'Oh, yes.' Nickolls had no difficulty in agreeing with such an estimate.

Frank Cassels asked no questions. Christmas Humphreys re-examined his witness and Nickolls agreed that at six feet it would be almost impossible to miss a man with Craig's gun. But, though it might follow that Craig had deliberately aimed at Fairfax, to hit Miles between the eyes at thirty-nine or forty feet must have been a fluke. However, Goddard intervened again to put a stop to the possibility of a plea of manslaughter.

'This revolver,' he asked, 'if it is fired off, and even if it is fired indiscriminately, is quite capable of killing people?'

'Yes,' said Nickolls, 'It is capable of being lethal.'

And Goddard added, for the benefit of the jury, 'No matter whether it is accurate or inaccurate.'

Humphreys, knowing perfectly well that Parris would pursue the manslaughter argument that Craig had fired at random and could not have done otherwise with an inaccurate weapon, questioned Nickolls further. Even at forty feet, if Craig fired repeatedly, would he not sooner or later hit someone? Nickolls would only say that it would be 'an extremely dangerous thing to do.'

Goddard intervened again to remind Humphreys that the law offered special protection to officers of justice. This was a case in which Miles, acting as an officer of justice, had been murdered. Then Goddard apparently realised what he had said. It was for the jury to decide whether Miles had been murdered or not. Goddard hastily corrected the word to 'shot.' Humphreys replied that he appreciated the position but he was anticipating what he thought would be the defence offered on Craig's behalf.

'Well,' said Goddard dismissively, 'if that defence is run, I shall tell the jury that that is no defence at all.'

And so, it seemed, the Lord Chief Justice had torpedoed John Parris's argument even before the defence case had been opened, let alone heard. Moreover, it had been done in the presence of the jury, as if for better effect. There was little more that Christmas Humphreys needed to do. Goddard had ruled out the only conceivable mitigation.

'My lord,' said Humphreys, 'that is the case for the prosecution.'

Just over twenty-four hours after making his Old Bailey debut in a case of the greatest importance, John Parris rose to begin the defence of Christopher Craig by putting the defendant in the witness-box. Given the overt hostility of the Lord Chief Justice in his remarks to Parris and in ruling out the proposed defence, the circumstances of that debut could scarcely have been more daunting.

Craig, permitted by Goddard to sit down while giving evidence, showed little bravado in the witness-box. Indeed, to judge from Goddard's early interjections,'What?' and 'What do you say?' he spoke so quietly that it was hard to hear him. Several times after that he was urged to speak up. He told his story straightforwardly, in answer to Parris's questions. He had been interested in guns since he was eleven and, in five years, he had owned forty or fifty of them. He had 'swapped them and bought them off boys at school.' About five other boys in the school used to have guns. There was no secrecy about this. Christopher Craig used to take weapons to school, 'to make myself look big, because I had got something they had not.'

Goddard was growing impatient of this recital from childhood experience. He interrupted Parris's questions with one of his own, addressed to Craig.

'Did you know that firearms could kill people?'

'Yes, sir,' said Craig. How could he not know it?

'Let us get on to something that matters,' said the Lord Chief Justice irritably.

Even so, Parris was not to be deflected. He asked about the Eley .455 and the sawing off of the barrel, which Craig had done to fit the revolver in his pocket so that he might take it to work and 'feel big.' He also asked about the boy's visits to the cinema. Craig answered that he went three or four times a week, to gangster films for preference.

Craig's version of events on the roof was that Fairfax grabbed Bentley, took him over to the staircase well-head and was then coming back for Craig. Bentley did not, according to Craig, shout, 'Let him have it, Chris!' Craig's intention was to frighten Fairfax away by firing into the ground. He did this, aiming at the surface of the roof a few feet in front of him. Fairfax would then have been almost forty feet from him. He saw that Fairfax had 'ducked to the ground' and Craig fired again over the side of the roof 'to frighten him off.'

'You fired another to frighten him off, did you?' Goddard asked.

'Yes, sir.'

'How many times do you say you fired altogether?'

'Nine, sir.'

'So you reloaded the revolver?'

'Yes.'

'Reloaded it,' Goddard repeated.

Then came the most important moment of all. The death of Sidney Miles, as described by his killer.

'The door flew open and I thought someone was rushing at me, sir. I saw someone was coming out, and I fired another one to frighten them away.'

Goddard took over the questioning.

'How did it come about that it hit PC Miles coming out of the door?'

'It might have ricochetted off. I do not know.'

'It might have ricochetted?'

'Ricochetted or anything, sir.'

Craig insisted that he had no intention of hitting anyone. It was all 'bluff.' He felt that he was 'in a film or something.' When he dived off the roof, he was upset by the knowledge that he had 'hurt' one of the policemen and wanted to kill himself. He remembered nothing from the moment that he began to fall until he woke up on the hospital trolley as someone hit him in the mouth and called him a 'murdering bastard.' As for his scornful comments in hospital during the days that followed, he could not remember making any of them.

Such was his defence. But Goddard had not let him finish without asking one further question.

'Have you ever expressed any regret or sorrow that you killed that officer?'

'Yes, sir.'

'When?'

'When I am in prison, sir.'

'Who to?'

'Not to anyone, sir.'

Craig's performance in the witness-box, when examined by his own counsel, had been less than convincing. But in cross-examination Christmas Humphreys treated him with the scorn and scepticism of an irascible schoolmaster confronting a proven delinquent.

'On this night you shot Police-Constable Miles,' Humphreys began, 'Is that right?'

'Yes.'

'And he died?'

'Yes.'

'You know that?'

'I found that out on Wednesday the fifth.'

'You meant to shoot him, didn't you?'

'No, sir.'

'You meant to shoot any police officer who tried to prevent your escaping from the felony you were committing?'

'I did not, sir.'

'Didn't you?'

'No.'

More and more, the scene resembled the headmaster's study where the moral anger of the pedagogue confronted adolescent subterfuge.

'Well,' said Christmas Humphreys, 'we will go into it.'

They went into it at considerable length. Craig admitted that he and Bentley had gone out that evening intending to break in and steal whatever they could get. He admitted that he was carrying the loaded gun and spare ammunition. The 'frolic' of running off to Brighton with another boy the year before began to seem less frolicsome when it was revealed that the companion had been carrying a Luger automatic, in addition to Craig's .45 Webley.

On the night of 2 November, Humphreys asked, did Craig set off with the loaded gun in his pocket? He did. And the knife? Craig admitted it. Humphreys asked for the knife and held it up. Where did Craig get it from? Craig said that he had bought it. Goddard intervened asking Craig twice what he carried the knife for. But Craig would only say that he always carried it and that it was 'only a sheath-knife.'

Then came the matter of the home-made knuckleduster with the spike on its edge. Craig agreed that he had given it to Bentley while they were on their way to commit the robbery. Goddard, taking the knuckleduster to examine it, asked Craig what the spike was for.

'I just put it in,' Craig said lamely, 'There was a hole.'

'What is it for?'

'I just put it there.'

'What is the knuckleduster for?'

'To put it on your hand, sir.'

'You put it on your hand to hit anybody?'

'Yes, sir.'

'What is this dreadful spike on it for?'

'That was in there, sir.'

'I know,' said Goddard, who was holding the knuckleduster as if to demonstrate it to the jury, 'but you say you made it. I want to know what you put this dreadful spike in for.'

'I didn't, sir. It was there. There was just a block of steel and I rounded off things and filed it.'

'So, if you have it on your knuckles, then you have got this as well?'

'Yes, sir.'

'A dreadful weapon,' said the Lord Chief Justice grimly.

The failing self-assurance of Craig's answers suggested that he was about to be brought to a halt in the witness-box. Presently, Humphreys turned to the question of whether Bentley knew Craig was carrying a gun. Goddard intervened and asked the question outright. Craig replied that he had not told Bentley about the gun. With some scepticism, Goddard asked whether they were going out to do 'this shopbreaking' together and yet Craig had said nothing about the gun. Craig could not summon up an answer.

In reply to Humphreys, Craig said that he had told Bentley about the loaded gun when he first saw the police. He denied the truth of Bentley's alleged comment, 'I told the silly bugger not to use it.' Goddard asked why Craig had told Bentley about the gun at that moment. Was it a reassurance that he would use it to keep the police off? Craig denied this.

'Then why did you tell him you had got it?'

'I don't know, sir.'

'You do not know!' said Goddard scornfully.

Goddard and Humphreys between them had routed the

sixteen-year-old Craig. His self-defence seemed of the feeblest, and he had incriminated his companion by saying that Bentley knew of the gun before Fairfax reached them. He insisted that he had not aimed at Miles or the staircase door but had fired over the garden of 30 Tamworth Road, adjoining the warehouse. Humphreys pointed out that, if that were so, Miles was in his line of fire. Given the inaccuracy of the gun, it was possible. Presently Craig repeated that he had lost consciousness as he dived from the roof. Then he insisted that he had fallen on his head and broken his back. Goddard demanded how he knew he had fallen in this way, if he was unconscious, 'Because I'm quite a good diver,' Craig said, 'and I have been off a lot of heights.'

By the time that Humphreys sat down, Craig was reduced to not remembering his shouts to the police or his comments in hospital, and to insisting that he only fired to frighten the officers away. Goddard asked again whether he had expressed any remorse or regret for his actions. There were plenty of policemen by his hospital bed to whom he could have said something.

'I was not conscious,' Craig insisted, 'I was hardly conscious half the time, sir.'

'Hardly conscious!' said Goddard sharply, 'Don't talk such nonsense!'

And though Craig left the witness-box with a final answer to John Parris, 'I have never hurt anyone in my life, sir,' his defence had been demolished under cross-examination.

Far worse was the appearance of Bentley in the witness-box. The terms 'half-wit,' 'mentally subnormal' and their kind were used about him with some imprecision. He could not read the words of the oath and had to repeat them as they were read for him by the clerk of the court. This first impression was bad enough, but to match Bentley against the Lord Chief Justice and Senior Treasury Counsel was tantamount to feeding the Christians to the lions. Even in answering Frank Cassels for the defence, Bentley confined himself to short flat sentences which seemed to match a shrunken intelligence. Summing up his relationship with Craig after leaving school, he could only say, 'He came round. We got in a bit of trouble, and we were kept apart.'

To get Bentley's story in the witness-box was as difficult as it had been for the police to get a coherent statement from him. Hesitant and, no doubt, bewildered by having to respond to hostile questions, he seemed shifty and evasive. He could do no more than cling to simple denials, however unconvincing they might seem. For the most part, Cassels himself suggested what had happened, leaving Bentley to say 'Yes, sir,' or 'No, sir,' as the case might be. Launching out on his own, Bentley's comprehension and powers of expression floundered. His most ambitious account of his arrest was, 'Sergeant Fairfax come and took me sir, because I could not see nothing where I was standing and he come and took me, and walked me across the roof.'

He insisted that he did not know Craig was carrying a gun until the first shot was fired at Fairfax. And, of course, he still denied saying, 'Let him have it, Chris.' He repeated that he had made no effort to escape nor to strike Fairfax. Both Bentley and Craig gave evidence that it was Craig and not Bentley who made the remark about the gun being a .45 Colt with plenty of ammunition.

Bentley continued to deny saying, 'I told the silly bugger not to use it,' and 'I knew he had got a gun, but I didn't think he'd use it.' He insisted that the only question put to him at the time by the police was about the name of his companion on the roof. Goddard intervened occasionally during Cassels' examination of his client. He wanted to know why Bentley had followed Craig over the warehouse gate. Bentley kept saying, lamely, that he did not know. Later on, Goddard asked him when he first knew that they were going to try breaking in at the warehouse. After some evasion, Bentley replied that it was only after climbing the gate that he knew they would try to break in. Whatever Goddard's feelings, he dealt with Bentley more lightly than he had done with Craig.

In conclusion, Cassels asked his client three questions upon which his life now depended.

'You did not know until the first shot was fired that Craig was armed?'

'No, sir.'

'Did you at any time tell Craig to use the gun or to use violence towards the police?'

'No, sir.'

'Did you yourself at any time use any violence towards any of the police officers?'

'No, sir.'

Frank Cassels sat down. John Parris had no questions to put to the witness. Bentley was left to the mercy of Christmas Humphreys.

Without preliminaries, Humphreys pitched into Bentley. How long had he known Craig? Bentley said it was a matter of years. Had he known of Craig's 'mania' for guns? Bentley denied it. Humphreys, recalling Craig's own evidence, wondered how it was possible to know him so long and be unaware of such an enthusiasm. Bentley must have known that Craig was carrying a gun that night, even before it was fired. Bentley denied it.

'Then what he has told the jury is a lie, is it?'

'I think so.'

'You heard it, didn't you?'

'I did, sir.'

'That is untrue?'

'That is untrue.'

'And all that the police officers have said about your showing your knowledge of that gun is untrue?'

'All untrue, sir,' Bentley said.

How could he have said anything else? Yet to believe Bentley it was necessary to believe that all the police witnesses and Craig himself were lying. Bentley alone was telling the truth. Humphreys put this improbable state of affairs to him and Bentley blundered into a longer and less coherent explanation.

'Craig may have put something in the way of that answer. I do not know. He may have got muddled up.'

It seemed not to occur to Bentley that Craig's precise words would have been recorded in court. Again and again, as the evidence of police officers was put to him, Bentley was reduced to saying, 'That is untrue,' or 'That is quite untrue.' At the end of five minutes, Humphreys had made him sound like an habitual liar and, it seems, Bentley had hardly noticed it. He did not know that

Craig's gun was a .45 and that he had plenty of ammunition for it.

'You know now?' asked Goddard.

'Yes, sir.'

'What has happened to be true,' the Lord Chief Justice added, making the point plain.

Humphreys came to the statement that Bentley had made to the police.

'Look at your statement, will you?'

'It is no good my looking at that, sir.'

'He cannot read it,' Goddard reminded Humphreys. But Humphreys seemed to miss the point. He read out part of the statement and asked Bentley why, if he now denied saying some of the things in it, he had signed it as true after it was read out to him. Bentley explained that he could not tell what he was signing, as he could have done if he had been able to read it. It was a reasonable argument, except that his denial required the jury to believe two more policemen were lying while Bentley alone told the truth.

In any case, Goddard had not finished with him yet. Bentley said that he remembered hearing Craig fire three shots. Goddard inquired, 'Did you shout out, "For God's sake don't fire," or "Shut up doing that," at any of those shots?'

'I don't remember, sir.'

Goddard passed the questioning back to Humphreys. In the next few moments, the noose was tightened round Bentley's throat without the prisoner understanding how or why.

'You did not tell him to stop because the place was surrounded?' Humphreys asked.

'I did not say nothing,' Bentley replied.

'According to you, when you were over by the staircase head, you were not being held by the police officer. Is that right?'

'That is right.'

'So that you were not under arrest at the time?'

'I was standing there, sir.'

'But you were not being held?'

'No,' said Bentley, not even aware that the trap had been laid, let alone that he had now stepped into it. He was not being physically held at that moment when Fairfax helped McDonald on to the roof. To be held by the police was a synonym for being under arrest. And if Bentley, by his simple-minded answer, was saying that he was not under arrest when Miles was killed, then he was fully and freely responsible with Craig for the murder.

Humphreys had got him and, moreover, had demolished any real hope of an appeal against conviction.

In a final display of moral anger before the jury, Humphreys made his denunciation of Bentley, and accused him of inciting Craig to fire again by shouting out, 'Look out, Chris, they're taking me down!' as he was led to the stairway after Miles had been killed.

'That was in case he shot me, sir,' Bentley explained.

'You were only thinking of your own skin, you mean?' Humphreys sneered at him.

Bentley tried to rephrase his explanation.

'If he shot me, there were two other police officers with me.'

But Humphreys, as if scenting a kill, would not let it go.

'You were frightened he might shoot at the police and hit you by mistake?'

'He might have hit anybody,' Bentley said plaintively. And that was certainly the truth.

Humphreys altered the final attack a little, suggesting that, when Bentley was being taken down, his words were an incitement to Craig to shoot so that he might escape.

'If I had done as you said, sir, I might have been shot myself.'

At last it was Bentley who seemed clearly to be speaking the truth and Humphreys who was reduced to an innuendo that sounded less than convincing. But it was too late to do any good. Dismissing the last answer, Humphreys said,

'I see. Still thinking of your own skin. In other words, you were prepared to assist Craig by such hitting with knuckledusters, or stabbing with daggers, or shooting with a revolver at the police as would enable you to escape if caught in the crime that you were committing.'

'No, sir,' Bentley said.

With that, Humphreys sat down. The task of cross-examining

Bentley had been almost too easy. As R. T. Paget later remarked, Humphreys had no need to make a fool of Derek Bentley, since God had already done that. But if this had been a circus entertainment of the Christian thrown to the lion, the Christian had quite unexpectedly at the final moment bitten his tormentor. The argument that Bentley was 'thinking of his own skin' and the harping on this carried no true power.

The general effect of the cross-examination had been devastating and Goddard's clerk, Arthur Smith, remembered Bentley looking like 'a zombie' at the end. As he was led back to the dock, the time for the lunch adjournment was approaching. Frank Cassels announced that he would call no further evidence. Bentley's parents were waiting outside to be called, in order to give evidence as to their son's medical history and mental capacity. There was other evidence of Bentley's mental condition that might have been called. But in that case, Cassels would have forfeited to the prosecution the right to make the final speech to the jury. He chose to leave his case as it was.

Goddard dismissed the jurors to an early lunch in order to hear legal arguments as to whether a verdict of manslaughter was possible. He had already suggested that it was not. John Parris began by citing two cases, the most recent in 1940, where it was ruled that the killing of a police officer, if unintentional, was manslaughter rather than murder.

The discussion did not last long. There was no need for Christmas Humphreys to argue alone against Parris's proposition since Goddard was doing that from the start. Craig, Goddard said, was by his own admission firing a revolver to frighten off the police. 'That is not an accident.' Humphreys added that the two accused had admitted their intention of breaking into the building and knowing that Fairfax was a policeman before a shot had been fired. Craig, as reported by Detective-Sergeant Shepherd, had said, 'I fired at a policeman.' Craig had hit two policemen out of nine shots fired.

As the argument developed, Parris's difficulty was not in demonstrating that manslaughter might occur when a policeman was killed. It was his attempt to show that Craig had not intended to hit Fairfax and Miles which seemed a lost cause. Everything that Craig had said and done appeared to prove that he had acted deliberately.

Craig's final hope of a manslaughter verdict vanished when Goddard read out extracts from other authorities, who took the view that even the accidental killing of a policeman was murder. In any case, Goddard repeated, the deliberate firing of a gun, with whatever purpose, could not be accidental.

'Does a man accidentally cause an injury if he runs down a street firing a gun? Although he is not firing at anybody, is that an accidental injury?'

Where did this leave Bentley? In order that he should be convicted, Goddard said, he must be aware that Craig was armed and the jury must be satisfied that he intended with Craig to offer violent resistance.

With that, the court rose and the spectators filed out to join the throngs of office workers in the misty lunch-hour of a cold December day. Already the attention of the press had begun to turn to the greater drama of life and death that must follow the trial.

The defence had called no witnesses apart from the two accused and it was therefore Frank Cassels and John Parris who were entitled to have the last word to the jury before Goddard's summing up. When the court sat again after lunch, Christmas Humphreys made the closing speech for the prosecution. He promised to be 'quite brief.' Speaking rapidly, he had finished within half an hour.

Humphreys returned to the point that Craig's crime would only be manslaughter if it was accidental. But Craig's comments, reported by several police officers, showed that he had tried deliberately to kill his victim and regretted only that he had not killed others. Craig denied this. In that case, either the police officers or Craig were not telling the truth. Which was it to be? The expressions on the faces of the jury answered that. Craig murdered Miles. He tried to murder Fairfax. He fired two bullets at PC Harrison perched on the roof. In each case he fired in a different direction. 'Out of nine bullets that he fires, he hits two human beings, and there is a not very wide miss of a third helpless target lying on the roof. This is his story. Do you believe it? I say no more upon the case concerning Craig. I ask you to say it is beyond argument.'

Bentley, uncomprehending and blundering in the witness-box, had destroyed his own case. With apparent fair-mindedness, Humphreys explained how he had tried to give Bentley the benefit of the doubt by suggesting that he was physically under arrest at the time of the murder. 'Bentley will not have it. Bentley is saying he was not, that he was not being held, that he was free to get away.' So far as the defence of being under arrest at the time of the murder went, said Humphreys, Bentley 'has knocked it from under his feet.' That was true. On the other hand, he had received invitation and encouragement from Humphreys to do it.

Eventually, it was a lawyer and Member of Parliament, Reginald Paget, who put the matter as Goddard should have done long before.

> Mr Humphreys, in opening the case for the Crown, had said Bentley was under arrest; every policeman had said Bentley was under arrest. The fact, beyond peradventure, was that Bentley was under arrest. What did it matter what this near half-witted boy said as to being under arrest?

In their final speeches, both John Parris and Frank Cassels spoke at far greater length on behalf of their clients than Humphreys had done for the prosecution, addressing the jury for almost an hour each. It was no disparagement of either to say that their efforts were doomed at the outset. Parris warned the jury against Humphreys' manner of sensationalising the case in comments better suited to a popular newspaper than a court of law. He cited one of them, 'Craig gloried in murder,' which the press had picked up immediately.

There were only two things that Parris could do and he did them as eloquently as possible. First he invited sympathy for Craig as the product of a troubled society.

'The tragedy of this trial is that Christopher Craig has become a symbol of wayward youth. The nation's uneasiness and anxiety about the state of their youth has been focused upon him.' By way of explanation, Parris denounced the malign influences of popular culture upon his client, a defence that was to be pressed into service in many a tight corner.

'There has been a most deplorable alteration in the conditions in which young people are brought up in these days. The influence of the films, and particularly the American gangster films, is corrupting the youth of our nation and is putting ideas into their heads that never would be there but for this constant influence on them.'

That at least was open to question. But Parris insisted that Craig was more the victim of the cinema because he could not read and therefore relied upon it for his entertainment.

Parris's second task was to persuade the jury that Craig was guilty of manslaughter but not of murder. In this he had to contend with the opposition of both the prosecuting counsel and the judge. Before the end of his speech, Goddard interrupted him to tell him that what he was saying and what the jury was hearing 'is not the law.' When Parris referred to the case in 1940, Goddard said bluntly, 'You have misread it.'

Cassels, in turn, tried to repair some of the damage done to his case by the performance of his client in the witness-box. He also corrected Humphreys' extravagant use of language, pointing out that what Humphreys had just called 'a murderous dagger' in Bentley's possession was in fact 'a small sheath-knife.' It was no more murderous in itself than a good many kitchen implements.

For the rest, he could only repeat the story that Bentley and Craig were agreed to commit theft. But Bentley had no prior knowledge that Craig was carrying the gun. Bentley was under arrest before Miles was killed and made no attempt to escape. True, he did not shout at Craig to persuade him to give himself up. But nor did he encourage him. When free to escape, said Cassels, there was no suggestion that Bentley shouted at Craig something like, 'Hold on a moment. I'm coming to you,' or 'Wait till I get out of the way.' He acted throughout like a man who had surrendered.

As for the disputed incitement, 'Let him have it, Chris,' would

Bentley have acted as he did if he had used these words in the sense alleged? Surely, if he had spoken them as an incitement and Craig had then shot Fairfax, Bentley would have taken the chance to escape. But when Fairfax got up again, he was still standing close enough for the policeman to punch him and grab hold of him again.

The intentions of Derek Bentley were far more an issue in the case than those of Craig. There was surely an argument for his innocence of murder and certainly for his innocence of any intention to murder. Frank Cassels did not invite the jury, as John Parris had done, to convict his client of the lesser charge of manslaughter. He asked them to find Bentley not guilty.

Ironically, Bentley's defence might have been easier had he admitted saying the things alleged by the police but, at the same time, putting his own explanation on them. Even the remarks alleged did not necessarily prove that he knew Craig was carrying a gun.

'Let him have it, Chris,' could well have meant, 'Hit him,' or 'Punch him,' or 'Get him off me,' rather than 'Shoot him.'

'It's a .45 Colt,' spoken after Craig began to fire, might simply have meant that Bentley and most of Craig's friends knew he possessed the gun and ammunition for it. If he was firing, that must be what he was using. It did not in itself mean that Bentley knew beforehand he was carrying it that night.

'I told the silly bugger not to use it,' was certainly capable of meaning, 'I told him, before this evening, never to use it,' or 'I told him not to bring it.' Again, it did not mean incontrovertibly that Bentley knew Craig was carrying it on that occasion.

'I knew he had a gun, but I didn't think he'd use it,' allegedly said in the police-car, was certainly capable of meaning, 'I knew he owned a gun but I didn't think he'd bring it and use it tonight.'

Bentley's enfeebled self-expression left such possibilities in the dark. Far worse, having denied that he said such things, he was reduced to his litany of 'Untrue, sir... Quite untrue...' when the sworn testimony of five police officers was put to him in the witness-box. Next day the jury must decide whom to believe. Would it be the policemen, soon to be commended and decorated for their bravery, or a self-confessed petty criminal?

When the speeches for the defence were over, Goddard adjourned the hearing until 10.30 the next morning. The wheel of judicial roulette had been spun. For Bentley, at least, it was all or nothing.

CHAPTER 13

It was over by lunchtime. Goddard summed up the evidence for three quarters of an hour. He dismissed the argument that films or comics were to be held responsible for the actions of the accused. Such things had 'very little' to do with the crime. It was idle to pretend, he said, that a boy of sixteen did not know the wickedness of taking a revolver and ammunition and firing it at someone. Films and comics were no excuse. Nor was the defence of manslaughter allowed to go further on Craig's behalf. The shooting of Sidney Miles was 'a deliberate act, a wilful act.' After that, he suggested to the jury, 'it may be that you will have some difficulty, as I do not hesitate to say that I have, in understanding what defence there can be in the case of the prisoner Craig.'

As he described the death of PC Miles to the jury, Goddard's language took on the drama and colour of the prosecution's.

'The aiming does not seem to have been bad, does it? Three shots, two police officers hit, one fortunately slightly, the other hit between the eyes, so that blood gushed out and he fell dead instantaneously.'

John Parris rose at the end of the summing up and pointed out that this was not what the police witnesses had said. There had been six or seven shots before Miles was hit.

'I have not got that, but it may be so,' Goddard said, looking at his notes, 'I do not know that it very much matters.'

In dealing with Bentley's case, Goddard compared the two defendants to a pair of housebreakers. One goes into the building, the other keeps watch outside. Would it not be absurd to acquit the one outside on the grounds that he did not actually set foot on the premises? If Bentley knew Craig was carrying the gun and was prepared to use it, there could be no defence in saying that he did not think Craig would go as far as he did. Bentley, of course, insisted that he did not know of the gun. But Goddard suggested that they would 'surely' conclude that when the two set off on their robbery, Craig's first words to Bentley would have been, 'It's all right. I've got a revolver with me.'

In the next few minutes, the Lord Chief Justice put on a performance that brought a good deal of criticism upon him.

'Where is that knuckleduster?' he asked, and it was handed to him. He turned to the jury again. 'Have you ever seen a more horrible sort of weapon? You know, this is to hit a person in the face who comes at you. You grasp it here, your fingers go through. I cannot quite get mine through, I think. And you have got a dreadful heavy steel bar to strike anybody with. And you can kill a person with this, of course. Then, did you ever see a more shocking thing than that? You have got a spike with which you can jab anybody who comes at you. If the blow with the steel is not enough, you have got this spike at the side to jab. You can have it to see, if you like, when you go to your room.'

Exactly why the jurors should need to contemplate the knuckleduster while deciding Bentley's guilt or innocence was not clear. But Goddard's demonstration was not yet over.

'Hand me that sheath-knife – the big one. One wonders really what parents can be about these days! Allowing a boy of sixteen – they say perhaps they do not know but why do they not know? – to have a weapon like this which he takes about with him?'

Bentley was not forgotten, however.

'Where is the other knife? Here is Bentley with a smaller knife, but you can feel it is sharp and pointed. What is he carrying that with him for in his coat, not even with a sheath on it? Can you believe it for a moment, although Bentley has said that he did not know Craig had a gun?'

The conclusion in common sense, Goddard insisted, was 'overwhelming.' Bentley knew Craig was carrying the revolver. Under arrest or not, he was guilty. Under arrest or not, he was liable to hang. The display of weapons and the emotive outburst, which had little to do with a direct summing-up of the case, was aimed at that. Even by the standards of Goddard's court appearances, it was a dramatic example of judicial indignation.

As for the conflict of evidence between Bentley and the police, who would believe Bentley now? The police officers, said Goddard, had shown conspicuous gallantry. 'Are you going to say they are conspicuous liars?' No nonsense about misunderstanding or misinterpretation. Once again, for Goddard, it was all or nothing. Had these officers come into the witness-box and sworn upon the Bible to facts they knew were untrue? They were men who 'on the night showed a devotion to duty for which they are entitled to the thanks of the community.'

For the defence, the outlook was as bleak as it could be. If Bentley knew Craig was carrying a gun and might resist arrest, Goddard concluded, 'Bentley is as guilty as Craig. He is as guilty in law as Craig.'

But that was not quite all. The aftermath of a good many trials might have been characterised by dissension and acrimony but at least there was agreement as to what had been said in court by the participants. According to the official transcript, Goddard's last instruction to the jury was, 'if you find good ground for convicting them, it is your duty to do so.' But John Parris and some of the journalists who were listening heard a different version. As he leant towards the jury, Goddard said slowly and deliberately, 'Unless you find good ground for not convicting them, it is your duty to do it.' Such an instruction, transferring the benefit of the doubt from the accused to the prosecution would have been at least astonishing and to many people improper.

It was 11.15 when Goddard sent the jury out to consider their verdict. He asked them if they would like to take any of the exhibits with them, the assorted weaponry of the two accused. He was not best pleased when the foreman asked instead for Sergeant Fairfax's coat and waistcoat. Goddard allowed it, with a gruff reminder that they were to consider the murder of PC Miles and not the wounding of Fairfax. His displeasure was caused by an indication that the jurors were prepared to consider Craig's version of the shot having been fired at a distance and having hit Fairfax by virtue of a ricochet. In that case, their minds were still open as to whether Craig or Fairfax had given a true account of that incident.

An hour and a quarter passed before the jury came back. But events moved on in No. 2 court. Norman Parsley was put up, for his part in the robbery of Mr and Mrs Howes. The evidence was heard and Goddard sent him down for four years. Parsley's counsel explained that his client had won a scholarship to Whitgift school and that there was a place waiting for him with a firm who were prepared to pay for his university education. He had not known Craig for long, having met him during the summer holidays. It was also said on his behalf that Craig had tried to get him to go along for the break-in at Tamworth Road but that Parsley had taken fright after his experience with Mr and Mrs Howes and had refused. Unfortunately, this was balanced by police evidence of finding a gun when Parsley's home was searched. Goddard informed the boy that, had he been over twenty-one, he would have gone down for twelve years

At length the jury in the murder trial signalled that they had reached agreement. Bentley and Craig were brought up from the cells. The Bentley parents who sat throughout the trial outside the courtroom, in expectation of being called on behalf of their son, were now ushered in as well

Goddard took his seat again and there was silence as the clerk of the court asked the foreman of the jury to confirm that its members were agreed. They were. Did they find Christopher Craig guilty or not guilty of murder?

'Guilty.'

Did they find Derek William Bentley guilty or not guilty of murder?

'Guilty,' said the foreman, 'with a recommendation to mercy.'

The brandishing of the knuckleduster and the knives from the judicial bench had not quite done its worst.

While Mr and Mrs Bentley sat stunned by his words, Goddard addressed their son, the little square cloth of the 'black cap' upon his wig.

'Derek William Bentley, you are nineteen years of age. It is my duty to pass upon you the only sentence which the law can pass for the crime of wilful murder. The sentence of the court upon you is that you be taken from this place to a lawful prison, and thence to a place of execution, and there you suffer death by hanging, and that your body be buried within the precincts of the prison in which you shall have been last confined before your execution. And may the Lord have mercy upon your soul.'

Mrs Bentley, when she recovered from her initial shock, began to weep. Goddard looked up at the warders in the dock.

'Take him down,' he said.

The press reported that Bentley 'nonchalantly hitched his trousers on his first few steps towards the condemned cell at Wandsworth.' To impartial observers, he seemed not so much nonchalant as shell-shocked. When he had been led down to the cells, Goddard turned to Craig. At sixteen, Craig could be sentenced to no more than indefinite detention during Her Majesty's pleasure. Goddard did this.

'Your heart was filled with hate,' he told Craig, 'and you murdered a policeman without thought of his wife, his family, or himself. And never once have you expressed a word of sorrow for what you have done... In my opinion, you are one of the most dangerous young criminals who has ever stood in the dock.'

Craig, in turn, was taken down to the cells. As he stood for a last moment before the court, he smiled, which was assumed to be the callous triumph of the killer who had 'cheated' the noose. As it happened, he was smiling at his parents sitting below him. Goddard asked Sergeant Fairfax, PC McDonald and PC Harrison to step forward. He bestowed 'the highest commendation' on the men of 'Z' Division, Metropolitan Police, for their conduct on the night of 2 November. His specific commendation went to Fairfax, McDonald, and Harrison for their courage. 'The thanks of all law-abiding citizens ought to be tendered to you.'

The thanks took a more tangible form on 6 January 1953 when Fairfax was awarded the George Cross, the highest civilian award for bravery in time of peace. McDonald and Harrison received the George Medal and PC Jaggs the British Empire Medal. The King's Police Medal was awarded posthumously to Sidney Miles and presented to his widow by the Queen.

But in the immediate sequel to the case, the interest of the press was in the phenomenon of Craig, the ruthless and unrepentant gangster of sixteen. Bentley had been sentenced to death but the recommendation to mercy was likely to save him. Goddard had concurred in this and said, in passing sentence on Craig, that he would forward the jury's recommendation to the Home Secretary. Of those recommended to mercy by juries in murder trials of the twentieth century, three quarters had been reprieved.

Reprieves were likely in cases where the principal culprit could not be hanged by virtue of age or insanity. This would be the more likely when the defendant under sentence had been an accomplice whose hand did not actually commit the murder.

There was also the question of Bentley's age, at nineteen and a half years old. Bentley was old enough to hang but only by a year or so. His youth would surely count in his favour. Though not mentioned much at the trial, his mental condition would also be an important factor in the Home Secretary's discussions and considerations. Bentley was not, in any legal sense, insane. But he was demonstrably feeble-minded and an epileptic. All things considered, there was ample reason to exercise the prerogative of mercy.

Goddard himself seems to have thought at first that Bentley would be reprieved. He went home from the Old Bailey that day and his housekeeper helped him off with his coat. She had thought it unfair that the life of the greater wrongdoer would be spared while that of the lesser criminal was forfeit.

'Well, I had to sentence him to death,' Goddard said to her, 'But don't worry. He won't be hung.'

Yet that was not a thought that gave him much comfort. In January 1962, interviewed by Fenton Bressler, he conceded that Craig's offence was the greater but 'both were equally guilty of murder and should equally have hanged.' Craig's own age had prevented that but, 'Because they couldn't hang the one doesn't mean to say they shouldn't have hung the other.'

But would they? The answer lay with Sir David Maxwell Fyfe. In his deliberations, he would have at his disposal Goddard's own observations, the jury's recommendation, and a variety of reports on Bentley's history and medical condition. There was much, but not everything, in that to urge a reprieve.

For the time being, the press had what it wanted for the next morning's headlines. FORTY-GUN CRAIG ... THE BOY KILLER ... A SYMBOL OF WAYWARD YOUTH ... 'HOW LONG AM I IN FOR?' CRAIG ASKS ... The reports told the story of the Craig Gang in Croydon and reporters interviewed boys from Norbury Secondary Modern. Craig held centre stage and Bentley was edged aside. There was an inquiry into the film that Craig had been to see a few hours before the shooting, *My Death is a Mockery*. Tame stuff it sounded even in 1952 and the blow-ups in papers like the *News Chronicle* of its leading actors produced only the homely and reassuring names of Donald Houston, Bill Kerr and Kathleen Byron. Still more surreal were reports from papers like the *Telegraph* that, 'The 300 boys at Norbury Manor School, where Craig was a pupil, have been warned that anyone found with a gun will be severely punished.' What the public was urged to think of as a wave of Chicago-style violence was to be turned back by a hundred lines or the headmaster's cane.

John Parris discovered that his client's parents had been hurried off by their *Sunday Pictorial* minder for a champagne dinner at Wapping. From there they were taken down to the Angel at Shepperton, where they were to stay until their story had been written. Among the other guests was the American film actor, Alan Ladd, in England for the opening of his new film, *The Iron Mistress*. Mrs Craig acquired his autograph.

Mr and Mrs Bentley went home to their younger son and daughter. No one yet showed much interest in them. They had no glamour and the procedures of the law were as incomprehensible to them as the etiquette of the remotest African tribe. Their son had been sentenced to hang. But they began to receive assurances from people who knew about such things that the sentence would not, of course, be carried out.

They went to visit him at Wandsworth prison, where he was now in the death cell. Parents and son talked across a table and a wooden partition that hid the lower half of each speaker. Even the warders seemed to encourage them in their hope. Something was said about the work that Derek Bentley would do once he was transferred to normal prison routine. Would the officers say such things unless they also thought that he was certain to be reprieved? Surely not.

There was, at last, something to feel cheerful about. Mrs Bentley decided to take her son some fruit at Christmas, rather as she might have done if he was in an approved school once again. When she did so she was made to take it away again. Food from outside the prison was not permitted. But still there was hope.

On that evening after the trial ended, as Lord Goddard was helped off with his coat and the *Sunday Pictorial's* Harry Proctor smiled at the Craigs over his champagne glass, it seemed that there was probably not a man or woman in England who thought that Derek Bentley would be put to death. But at this stage, only the thoughts of one man could determine that, Sir David Maxwell Fyfe. The Bentley family did not yet know it, but its innocent members were about to undergo weeks of what they afterwards called 'torture' at the hands of Maxwell Fyfe and the system of justice that he represented. 'The man who rations mercy,' as he was called, was not in the mood to show softness to the young criminals whose violent acts had filled the press for several months past.

CHAPTER 14

It was not to be expected that the Home Secretary would say anything immediately in Bentley's case. Craig's defence had been exhausted, but for Bentley there was the hope of a successful outcome in the Court of Criminal Appeal. Frank Cassels based the appeal on two grounds. First, Goddard had not properly put Bentley's case to the jury in his summing-up. Second, Goddard had not invited the jury to consider how long after Bentley's arrest it was reasonable to suppose that he and Craig remained in 'concerted' action. However unfavourable a limit might be put upon this, the fact that there could be a limit should have been suggested to the jury.

Craig had already begun to serve his sentence, for the most part of it in Wakefield prison. He was released on licence in 1963, having been a model prisoner. He settled in the Home Counties, married, became an engineer and rejoined the ranks of the law-abiding. His career as a sardonic teenage gunman had been remarkably short, about a year in all. Despite the high drama in the newspaper headlines, Christopher Craig in retrospect had the appearance of a difficult adolescent. A good many of his contemporaries came very close to a similar fate. But the guns they fired hit no one and the crimes they committed were written off as casual bullying or petty larceny. As Craig was driven away to prison, there but for the Grace of God or the laws of coincidence, would have gone a good many more adolescent sons of the bourgeoisie.

By Christmas 1952, Craig had played his part in the drama. Bentley remained in the public eye, but for a week or so that eye was firmly upon the merry slaughter of poultry and pigs in order to load the dining-tables of the nation during the season of good will. As 1952 drew to its close, the nation had got used to the idea that George VI was dead and a new reign had begun. It was more than a new reign, for there were signs of a new Elizabethan age. The story of the Croydon shooting and its aftermath was submerged in the growing enthusiasm for the great summer coronation that might usher in a post-war age of golden achievement. And then, by the time that the world woke from its late December lethargy and the New Year of 1953 was rung in, it was almost time for Bentley's appeal.

The appeal was heard on 13 January. Bentley, wearing a grey coat over his suit, was guarded by three warders throughout the proceedings. Mr Justice Croom-Johnson, a veteran of conservative instincts, was to hear the appeal, assisted by Justice Ormerod and Justice Pearson. Frank Cassels and Christmas Humphreys appeared for the two sides. For the most part, the debate was between Cassels and Croom-Johnson. Justice Ormerod said little and Justice Pearson nothing at all. Thanks to Bentley's blundering and uncomprehending performance in the witness-box, Humphreys had little enough to do during the proceedings, though he answered the argument briefly at the end.

The true significance of the appeal lay outside the particular legal arguments. The conviction of Bentley had set in motion that political and administrative machinery which, unless halted, would put him to death. The machinery was proverbially unresponsive. It was difficult to get it into motion, but once in motion it was equally difficult to halt it. A successful appeal was the one sure method.

Cassels came at once to the first ground of the appeal, that 'the learned judge failed adequately to put the Appellant's defence before the jury.' Bentley's defence, Cassels repeated, was his insistence that he did not know Craig had a gun and that he had never said that he did know it. In a summing-up of three-quarters of an hour, Goddard had given one sentence, which lasted for about twenty seconds, to explaining Bentley's defence to the jury. By contrast, he had spent about five minutes displaying the knives and knuckleduster to the jury, explaining the injuries that they might have caused if they had been used, and asking the jurors whether they would not care to have them in front of them while they considered their verdict. To that extent, what might have happened but did not had appeared more important than what actually did happen.

A number of those who witnessed Goddard's performance at the Old Bailey on that December morning thought his summing-up blatantly partial. But a general accusation of this kind would carry little weight with the Court of Criminal Appeal. Cassels was obliged to specify the virtual omission of Bentley's evidence from that summing-up. There was, for example, no reference to Bentley's denial of the conversation about Craig's gun in the police car though the police evidence was included.

Justice Ormerod stopped Cassels. Goddard had given one sentence to Bentley's evidence, the denial that he knew about the gun while still on the roof.

'Does not that cover it?' he asked, 'I agree it is short.'

The impression soon grew that the appeal judges had heard enough even before the argument was over.

'If the Chief Justice had gone into the Prosecution's case in the same short detail as he went into the Appellant's case, I should have no complaint,' said Cassels determinedly. He went on to point out that Bentley had given evidence to deny the accuracy of the written statement taken down by Detective-Sergeant Shepherd. Goddard ignored that denial in presenting his summary to the jury.

'Be it so,' said Croom-Johnson blandly, 'this is the sort of controversy that arises in a great number of cases. . . All that is for the jury, is it not?'

Cassels agreed that it was a decision for the jury as to whom they believed. But it was the duty of the trial judge to put the two versions of events clearly before them. Croom-Johnson was unhappy about this.

'You do not seem to leave much to the discretion of the trial judge, do you? Surely it is for the learned judge to decide what he is going to lay before the jury.'

Croom-Johnson added that the case must be laid 'fairly and squarely,' but there was no requirement beyond that. Indeed, he suggested, it would have been enough for Goddard to devote his summing-up to the case for the prosecution and then simply say, 'Remember that the prisoner denies it all,' Croom-Johnson added that he knew of no method of putting a controversy except in that way.

Cassels insisted that Bentley and the police witnesses gave different versions of the conversation in the police car. Croom-Johnson interrupted at once, saying that Cassels was not being 'accurate.' There were not two versions. The police said that Bentley admitted knowing about the gun, Bentley denied he had said anything of the sort. A denial was not a 'version' and did not need to be explained as such. As for the brevity with which Goddard put Bentley's defence, 'Very often a summarised form is much more likely to achieve justice than if you go into details.'

It was clear that Cassels' criticism of Goddard's summing-up of Bentley's case was getting nowhere. Perhaps there would be more sympathy for the second argument. Goddard had not put to the jury the possibility that when Bentley was arrested, quarter of an hour before the death of PC Miles, his 'joint enterprise' with Craig was at an end. Whether or not that was a valid point of law, the possibility of it should have been put to the jury. If, for example, Bentley had been taken to Croydon police station and was assisting the police before Craig fired the shot that killed Miles, he would hardly be part of a 'joint enterprise' then.

Croom-Johnson warned Cassels not to be lulled into 'a sense of false security.' The fact that Bentley was arrested did not necessarily put an end to the joint enterprise. Cassels agreed but insisted that Goddard had been wrong in not putting to the jury the possibility that the joint enterprise might be at an end with Bentley's arrest. Croom-Johnson echoed his earlier objection to such arguments.

'A judge in the course of summing up in a criminal trial cannot deal with every little point. The judge must be allowed a little latitude, mustn't he?'

The 'little point' at issue was no less than a matter of life and death to Derek Bentley, a main support of his defence. His denial of police evidence would do him no good. But if his joint responsibility with Craig ended at the point of his arrest, he might escape the gallows. Cassels conceded that the jury might dismiss the argument. But Goddard should have made them aware that the argument existed.

Unfortunately, Cassels had not only to contend with the unsympathetic response of the appeal judges. There was also the blundering performance of the uncomprehending and dim-witted Bentley in the witness-box. Fairfax had arrested him and taken him behind the staircase well-head. But what then? Bentley, said Cassels, 'at the time the fatal shot was fired, and for some considerable time before, was under arrest and being held by the police officer.'

'Bentley himself denied that on oath,' said Justice Ormerod, 'He was not being held at the time the fatal shot was fired.'

The trap, into which Bentley had stepped during Humphreys' cross-examination, still held him fast. When Fairfax went to assist McDonald on to the roof, he had left Bentley standing alone. Bentley admitted that, to show that he had made no attempt to escape.

'You were not under arrest at the time?' Humphreys had asked him, referring to the moment when Miles was killed. Bentley, who had seemed visibly to be fumbling for the right answer, could only say, 'I was standing there, sir.' He certainly did not confirm that he was under arrest. 'But were you not being held?' Humphreys had asked him. 'No, sir.' There was no need to hold Bentley. He was making no attempt to escape. The fact that he was not being held on to was no more a proof that he was not under arrest than if he had not been held on to at the police station. Had Bentley begun to struggle at this point he would most certainly have been deemed to be 'resisting arrest.' But the law had its own tricks and terminology. Bentley admitted that he was not being 'held,' as in being 'held for questioning.' The subtleties and the ambiguities of the word were beyond him. But the hesitant half-wit in the witness-box was considered to have denied being under arrest. In that case, he was still responsible for Craig's actions. And in that case, he would hang.

The procedures of law and government were to have a good

deal of such procedural sport with Bentley before they put him to death. Christmas Humphreys, replying to Cassels in the Court of Criminal Appeal, conceded that Bentley might seem to have been 'technically under arrest.' But, he added, 'I was amazed to find that the case for Bentley was that he was not under arrest and was free to go to the assistance of Craig and did not do so.' For that interpretation of the case, Bentley's blundering under cross-examination was largely responsible.

The three judges withdrew to consider their decision in the matter. When they returned, Croom-Johnson delivered their judgment. In summarising Bentley's evidence in a single sentence, 'The matter was carefully put, adequately put, and properly put by the Chief Justice.' The first ground of appeal offered by Cassels was dismissed.

As for the matter of whether Bentley was under arrest or not at the time of the murder – and whether Goddard had put this possibility properly to the jury – Croom-Johnson and his two companions seemed to be rather more intrigued by the macabre spectacle of Bentley putting the noose round his own neck with no idea that he was doing so.

'It is a little difficult for Mr Cassels,' Croom-Johnson said, savouring the irony of the situation, 'because his own client was asked specifically at the hearing whether he was under arrest at the time when this shot which killed Miles was fired. He would not have it. He said he had not been arrested, that he was not under arrest, that the police officer had not detained him, and all the rest of it.'

What Bentley had said was that no one was holding on to him at the moment Miles was shot. It was an imprecise reply. For his imperfect grasp of the English language, Bentley was likely to pay with his life. It was like the ghastly little grammar lessons favoured by teachers of the old school. 'I shall drown and no one will save me,' was a cry for help. 'I will drown and no one shall save me,' entitled the struggler to be left to his fate. Croom-Johnson sought to console Frank Cassels that his 'difficulty' was nothing out of the ordinary.

'The answers in cross-examination by an individual on trial do sometimes have the result of destroying the possibility of a good point of law being persisted in which the learned counsel has endeavoured to get on its feet before a jury.'

There was, therefore, no reason why Goddard should have suggested to the jury that Bentley was under arrest, if he considered that Bentley himself had denied it. The appeal, said Croom-Johnson, was one which was 'in our judgment, without foundation and which is accordingly dismissed.'

The proceedings had lasted for about an hour. To anyone happening to hear them with an innocent ear, they seemed an appalling blend of Lewis Carroll's Red Queen, a touch of 'justice' as dispensed sardonically by the courts of Erewhon, served up with the black irony of Jonathan Swift. Carroll, Samuel Butler, and Swift meant nothing to Derek Bentley. He knew only that he was now likely to be hanged.

The Attorney-General, Sir Lionel Heald, refused to allow Bentley a further appeal to the House of Lords, permitted if the Attorney-General himself considered that the case involved a point of law of exceptional public importance. The Bentley case did not seem important to him, in that respect. He and his government colleagues were about to find out that the public thought otherwise. However, so far as the process of law was concerned, Bentley had lost the argument once the appeal judges had spoken.

Goddard himself was under attack by Michael Foot in the *Daily Herald* for his reactionary outbursts. On 14 January 1953, when a Tory MP, Wing-Commander Eric Bullus, published a private member's bill to restore judicial flogging, Goddard's was seen as the influence behind it. Lord Chorley responded by saying that it was 'difficult for Englishmen not to feel ashamed' of the conduct of their Lord Chief Justice. In the House of Commons, Goddard was denounced by the Labour MP Fred Willey, who pointed out that parliament had abolished flogging after long consideration. He demanded, 'I would like to know who the Lord Chief Justice thinks he is.'

John Parris, free of the restraints imposed upon him as Craig's counsel, made a speech as prospective Labour candidate for

Bradford North on the evening of 18 January. He was fully reported in the *Yorkshire Post* and more briefly in a number of other papers. He accused Goddard of being like a certain cat, two-headed, and trying to play both judge and politician. The Lord Chief Justice had once been a prospective Conservative candidate, so his political loyalties were no secret. He attacked Goddard's questioned impartiality in the campaign to restore flogging. But, according to the *Yorkshire Post*, he also denounced Goddard's conduct in court. Or, rather, Parris used the trick that Cicero had perfected of enumerating the things that he would not say. As a member of the bar, it would be improper to denounce a judge publicly. 'Unfortunately I am precluded from expressing in public the universal consensus of opinion in the legal profession about the manner in which he conducts criminal trials.' Parris was subsequently censured by the Benchers of Gray's Inn for his comments and was suspended from practising at the bar for four months. After the way in which Goddard had treated him during the trial of Craig and Bentley, he may have felt that the price was worth it.

Goddard had been seen as the villain so far by those who were appalled at the way in which they thought Bentley was being bundled towards the gallows. After the appeal, it was announced by the Home Office that he would be hanged at Wandsworth on 28 January, just two weeks away. In Fairview Road, Norbury, the Bentley family realised that the courts and the law would do nothing for them. Their eldest son stood very nearly on the edge of the pit of destruction.

Where justice had failed them, there was still the hope of mercy. If ever a condemned man deserved it, Bentley was surely he. Among those who were young and not as yet cynical about political figures, there was still a feeling that Bentley would surely not hang. His guilt was a technicality. He had not killed PC Miles nor intended to. Even Mrs Miles, the policeman's widow, was said to be of the opinion that Bentley ought not to die for the murder of her husband.

It was not, of course, customary for a reprieve to be announced at once. There was much for the Home Secretary to consider.

Now that the appeal was over, he could consider it. Meanwhile, in Fairview Road, there began what William Bentley later called the weeks of 'Torture by Hope.' More accurately, it was hope repeatedly offered and then just as repeatedly withdrawn.

In the fortnight between the dismissal of the appeal and the execution date, the contest seemed to be between the Home Secretary and Bentley's family. Humphreys, having secured the verdict and the death sentence, withdrew to his Buddhism and other intellectual pleasures. He had done his job. When he published his memoirs, quarter of a century later, the case of Bentley and Craig was not so much as mentioned. They were Orwellian non-persons. Goddard moved on to other things. The newspapers lost interest. Bentley's counsel had done all that could reasonably be required of him. Coronation Year and its expected triumphs were on the road.

There remained only the wretched, mentally subnormal youth in the condemned cell at Wandsworth, still hoping that he might be transferred to some other prison to begin a life sentence. His parents visited him each day, hoping for good news to take him and finding none. They talked of his dogs and the television sets that his father had in to repair. The warders were kindly, so far as they could be, for it now became evident that the punishment of the family's innocent members was to be of the most appalling kind.

Maxwell Fyfe, in the Home Office, had yet to consider the case. By his own account, he left it until the week of 19 January, nine days before Bentley was to hang. Unfortunately, it was a week during which Maxwell Fyfe was also preoccupied by the debate over the development of iron and steel and tinplate works at Margam and Trostre, the subject of parliamentary business on 22 January. Bentley must wait until after that.

Maxwell Fyfe's conduct in the end was not of a kind to inspire admiration. He made it a good deal worse by the manner in which he subsequently wrote about it, revealing that the way in which he made his decision was almost more chilling than the decision itself. His own account of what he thought the case was about is a revelation of his indifference or incomprehension. He was under the impression on p.206 of his memoirs that Craig as well as Bentley had appealed. Indeed, he thought that Craig had been sentenced to death and then been reprieved because of his age. Perhaps that mattered little. He thought Bentley shouted, 'Give it him, Chris!' rather than 'Let him have it, Chris!' which might not have mattered much either, though all this says little for Maxwell Fyfe's attention to detail. Far more important, he thought that Bentley shouted the words, 'whereupon Craig shot and killed another police officer.' At first it sounds as if Maxwell Fyfe thought two policemen had been killed. This was not so. But he believed that the death of Miles followed at once and, hence, Bentley could not have been under arrest at that moment and Bentley deliberately and directly incited the killing.

It was possible that Maxwell Fyfe edited the facts in his memoirs so that his conduct might sound more reasonable. That would do him little credit. It is also possible that, contrary to his own account, he did not agonise in quite such detail over the decision.

'It is a bleak, solitary, miserable position for any sensitive or imaginative man,' he later wrote.

One might suppose he was referring to the youth who spent his last days and nights under the ever-watchful light of the death cell. Of course, he was not. Maxwell Fyfe was referring to himself and the burden of the decision he must make. Self-pity is the only kind of compassion that his account of the Bentley case emits.

Sensitivity was not Maxwell Fyfe's forte. Politicians are apt, to some degree, to be insulated by the trappings of office from the nuances of public feeling. None was ever more insulated than Maxwell Fyfe just then. He understood that in the last months of 1952 the press had headlined 'public concern' about violent crime and the near-hysterical belief in salvation by the birch or the noose. If Bentley were hanged, an example would be made and political capital might be garnered from that. Maxwell Fyfe did not yet understand that there was a growing alarm in the country at what seemed to be a callous and opportunist act of judicial murder. When he awoke to this, his tone suggested a peevish displeasure at the public's ingratitude for his firmness. He wrote later and still with bewilderment of events which 'brought down on my head a storm of vituperation without parallel in my career.' Of that storm there was no doubt.

Maxwell Fyfe also protested that he went to great lengths to see if there were not grounds for reprieving Bentley. He considered the evidence in the trial, medical reports, family circumstances, other private circumstances, police reports and 'available precedents.' Almost twenty years later, in David Yallop's account of the case, Lord Goddard revealed that Maxwell Fyfe had not bothered to consult him. Had there been such consultation, Goddard said, he would have recommended a reprieve.

One factor above all others preoccupied the Home Secretary, by his own account. The case involved the murder of a policeman. Maxwell Fyfe therefore considered 'the possible effects of my decision upon the police force.' This was soon unsympathetically described by R. T. Paget, Labour MP and QC, as 'a new doctrine that where a policeman is killed somebody must be hung.'

And so Maxwell Fyfe brooded. It was not merely, he said, a matter of examining legal, medical, and personal files. So what was it a matter of, from the point of view of the Home Secretary? He explained that too.

It cannot be emphasised too strongly that he is intervening in the due process of the law; to decide, in short, if those processes ought to be diverted. His decision may bring the law into public hatred or contempt, and this factor is of great – although not overriding – importance. And, in spite of the documents submitted to him and the advice available to him, the final decision is his alone.

It sounded, from those last words, as if Maxwell Fyfe had decided beforehand that Bentley must die. At least he seems to have thought that he would please the public more easily by not interfering in the 'process' of law. That he himself was part of that process seems not to have commended itself to him as a principle. By denying it, he had only to stand aside and let the hangman do his work for him.

His final comment will seem appealing, pathetic, cynical or obtuse, according to taste.

I am sure that most Home Secretaries have approached their decision as I did, with an overwhelming anxiety to find any factors which would justify a recommendation for mercy.

'Overwhelming anxiety' on Bentley's behalf and a search for 'any' favourable factors might soon have been satisfied. Many of the factors were public knowledge and others were well-known to Maxwell Fyfe himself.

The jury had recommended Bentley to mercy and Goddard had endorsed that recommendation. Three-quarters of all those convicted of murder in the twentieth century but recommended to mercy had been reprieved. These were men and women who, in almost every case, had actually committed the murder.

Bentley had not killed anyone, indeed he had no record of violence at all. The Commissioners of Criminal Law as far back as 1839 and the Royal Commission of 1878 had both recommended that offences such as Bentley's should be excluded from the category of murder. In reminding Maxwell Fyfe of this, Reginald Paget added that the law had not been altered 'because it was felt that the prerogative of mercy could be trusted to cover cases such as these.'

It was also the practice to reprieve a lesser accomplice if the person primarily responsible for the murder could not be executed by reason, for example, of youth or insanity.

The medical reports on Bentley made it plain that he was mentally subnormal almost to the verge of mental deficiency, and he was epileptic. On behalf of the Home Office, Dr Denis Hill of the Maudsley Hospital had examined Bentley before the trial and reported on his mental state. By any criterion, this would diminish his criminal responsibility while under the leadership of someone like Craig.

Maxwell Fyfe was not likely to criticise Goddard's handling of the case. On the other hand, it was quite clear that Bentley had destroyed his hope of a successful appeal by his vagueness in the witness-box as to whether he was under arrest or not when Miles was shot.

These were not the only considerations. There was also, for example, the matter of Bentley's youth. But for a Home Secretary who professed 'overwhelming anxiety' to find 'any' favourable factor to justify a reprieve, they were quite enough to be going on with. So many of them were generally known that, combined with a sense of natural justice, they persuaded the public not to worry on Bentley's behalf. 'At that stage,' wrote Paget later, 'nobody dreamed for a moment that Bentley was going to hang.'

There were still voices of moral indignation beyond the windows of the Home Office and the vista of Whitehall. Wing-Commander Bullus had his motion down for the restoration of flogging, while the women's groups and the political right wished him well. But the case of Bentley seemed to halt momentarily the tide of moral indignation. The satisfaction of communal repentance and self-righteousness, no less than lechery, is an indulgence that is apt to pall. The nation hungered for justice in the autumn of 1952, by courtesy of the press. But the bitter fogs of December and January seemed to have cooled its appetite.

Maxwell Fyfe, at the end of a fateful week, looked at the case of Derek Bentley. Everything at Wandsworth had been prepared for the hanging of the uncomprehending youth on the following Wednesday morning. The Bentley family had distributed petition-forms in the hope of getting a thousand signatures. Sir David Maxwell Fyfe, remembering the autumn, heard the cries of anger against the cosh-boys and cosh-girls, the young thugs and the teenage gunmen. And even if the crime statistics showed a decline in the number of offences, he insisted that the law must not be brought into 'public hatred or contempt.' Craig, after all, had 'got away with it' already by virtue of his age. What would the vigilantes and women say if Bentley 'got away with it' as well? What would the papers say about him? Worst of all, what would the police force say? He discussed the matter with his wife 'a lot' by her own account. Lady Maxwell Fyfe had urged the Conservative women at Rhyl to birch their children as necessary but this was her first excursion into the practicalities of capital punishment.

But, as Maxwell Fyfe wrote, even a few days of thinking about the Bentley case seemed like 'an interminable period.' By Saturday he had had enough of it. His mind was made up.

CHAPTER 15

'I shall now rely on public opinion to save my boy,' Mr Bentley had told the press as soon as the appeal was dismissed. Had public opinion been consulted, it would have saved Derek Bentley by a majority of at least three-to-one, if the letters and telegrams were anything to go by. But it was not a matter of public opinion. Bentley must live or die at the command of the Home Secretary, a man who misjudged the public mood by his own account but who cared little for it anyway when his misjudgment became clear. It was time to teach the violent young 'no end of a lesson.'

So far as Derek Bentley's parents, his brother and sister, were concerned Maxwell Fyfe kept up the 'torture by hope' for a little longer. By the last weekend before the execution date, Mrs Bentley was ill: the burden of the campaign fell upon her husband and her twenty-one-year-old daughter Iris. It was not only a matter of being sick with worry and fear. The Bentley family now found itself lost in a labyrinth of legal nicety, at the centre of which sat the Home Secretary and his advisers.

As the date for the hanging grew frighteningly close, the press realised that the Bentley story was, after all, going to beat the Craig story by a good margin. It offered human interest, pressed down and overflowing. How many parents read the morning editions and shuddered at the thought that their own teenage son, under the malign influence of a more powerful personality, might now be passing his final days playing cards with the warders of the death-watch?

Reporters from Fleet Street, Europe, the Commonwealth and even the United States began to take up the story. The press was gathering in Fairview Road and the phone in the Bentley house rang constantly. Quite apart from the lone plight of Derek

Bentley himself, the bewildered and frightened family became aware that there was sympathy for them on every side. The moral vigilantes who had spent the autumn assuring the nation that it needed to scour the Augean stables of films and books, that its judges must not spare youthful malefactors, never doubted what sort of family produced such delinquents. The parents were casual and indifferent. There was no discipline. Children were brought up on the easy criminal violence of the cinema screen and the comic book.

Now the vigilantes themselves came under question. At the time of PC Miles' murder, Lord Merthyr had told the press on 6 November that 'lack of discipline' was the root cause of adolescent delinquency. During the trial, on 8 December, *The Times* carried a feature on the same theme, JUVENILE CRIME – UNHAPPY HOME A MAIN FACTOR. But now the public discovered the truth of Derek Bentley's family background. Theory and fact proved ill-matched.

His family were decent, honourable, hard-working people. Ten years earlier, they would have been regarded as part of the backbone of England in its resistance of Nazi might. Mr Bentley was away in the army, his family endured the blitz stoically and had the experience of being bombed-out twice. Three members of the family died in the attacks. They were the epitome of 'London can take it.' Since then the parents, often under adverse material circumstances, had tried to do the best for their children. There had been moral standards and Sunday school. When Mr Bentley feared for his son, he acted like a responsible citizen by asking the police to help him. They had not been able to do so. As for the diet of crime, Bentley's last film had been a Betty Grable feature. His choice of television that Sunday night was an old-time music-hall selection, *The Passing Show*. Even those whose fingers had itched to lash out at the 'young thugs' and the 'cosh-boys' had an uneasy feeling that they had got the wrong culprit.

As soon as the appeal was dismissed, Mr Bentley and his well-wishers began to organise their petition. They would collect a thousand signatures and then take them to the Home Office, asking Maxwell Fyfe to reprieve Derek Bentley. The forms were issued. The petition for a reprieve circulated in the streets, in canteens and pubs. It was accompanied by a letter from Mr Bentley to what he described as 'the fair-minded British public.' Though the precise wording had been the work of one of Mr Bentley's advisers, the sentiments were his own.

We appeal to everyone in this country to give careful consideration to the following vital facts in the case of the State versus my son, Derek Bentley.
1. Derek had not been previously engaged on any crime of violence; he was not a hardened criminal; his only previous offence was a minor one for which he had paid.
2. On the night of the crime he was not armed.
3. If he acted in concert with Craig in the dastardly murder of PC Miles, why did he not make use of the knuckleduster to avoid being taken into custody?
4. At the time the shot was fired, he was held by Sergeant Fairfax.
5. He did not have any reason to hold any grudge against the police, as did Craig.
6. The words 'Let him have it, Chris,' if said, could have meant 'Let him have the gun.'
7. If he had not been taken into custody it is likely he may have deterred Craig from the act that has left my boy, and not Craig, in the shadows of the hangman's noose.
8. It had been argued by some that the law should be allowed to take its course in order to set an example to other wrong-doers, but in the name of British justice only why pick on my boy, who has been guilty of a technical offence?

It was possible to query the accuracy of certain points in the letter. It did not make clear, for example, in what sense Bentley was being 'held' at the time of the shot that killed Miles. However, it was not possible to query the response of ordinary men and women who had the petition presented to them in these terms. Some were appalled and some, who had lately demanded punishment and example, now had reason to feel stirrings of conscience. To Mr Bentley's astonishment, he found that in a short space of time he had not a thousand signatures to his petition but a hundred thousand.

On 18 January, Mr Bentley announced that one man who was dismayed at the course of events had printed 'BENTLEY MUST NOT DIE' car-stickers which would soon be seen everywhere. Mrs Bentley had written a personal letter to the Queen. Ironically, Coronation Week 1953 had been chosen as the date for Iris Bentley's wedding, in an impulse of patriotic sentiment. The money set aside for it, £300 all told, was now spent in trying to save the elder son from the representatives of Her Majesty's justice.

The house in Fairview Road was receiving sympathetic mail by the sackload. It was decided to empty the sacks into the bath and sort through the letters at leisure. On Friday 25 January, five days before the execution date, Mr Bentley and his daughter Iris set off for an appointment at the Home Office. As a sample, they took two parcels of the petition forms with eleven thousand signatures. They also took Mr Bentley's letter to the Home Secretary and a copy of his letter to the British public.

By the time that father and daughter arrived, reporters were outside the Home Office in strength. Mr Bentley and Iris were led to a room and met by a senior official who took the petition forms and the letters. He was, Mr Bentley recalled, courteous and sympathetic. More than that, he was evidently 'distressed.' He assured his visitors that any further signatures they received to their petition might be brought and added to the evidence for a reprieve. On the steps outside, William Bentley read out the contents of his public letter and made a statement.

'If the public feel that the facts I have just read out, together with the evidence at the trial, amounts to murder, then my son is guilty. If not, they should do everything in their power to stop the state taking the course it is now upon.'

On the following day, Saturday 24 January, there was an intervention from another direction. Before the Old Bailey trial, Bentley had been examined by Dr Denis Hill of the Maudsley Hospital. As if sensing that the medical evidence might be overlooked in considering a reprieve, Dr Hill wrote to the Home

Office, leaving its officials in no doubt as to Bentley's medical condition, specifically the fact that he was an epileptic. His letter evoked no response, other than that he was forbidden to make his concern public.

Mr Bentley, on the same day, received an enigmatic telegram from a woman in Southend, telling him that he must come at once to see her. He was driven to Southend in a hired car, where the elderly woman revealed to him that she was the sister of the Home Secretary. She had taken a great interest in the case, had prayed for the Bentley family night after night, and had written to her brother about the reprieve. She was now able to assure Mr Bentley that his son would not hang.

William Bentley was driven back to Norbury. He had not, apparently, been the victim of a deliberate hoax. But the woman was not the Home Secretary's sister. She was merely mad as a hatter.

On Monday morning, two days before the execution date, one of the reporters asked Mr Bentley whether it was true that Maxwell Fyfe had refused a reprieve. The Bentleys knew nothing about this. There would surely have been a telegram or a special message. They went up to the bathroom and sorted through that morning's post. Among the welter of envelopes there was one 'On Her Majesty's Service.' They opened it and read the contents. It had been signed by a senior Home Office official, Sir Frank Newsam, and sent on Saturday by ordinary post.

> I am directed by the Secretary of State to inform you that he has given careful consideration to the petition submitted by you on behalf of your son Derek Bentley, and I am to express to you his deep regret that after considering all the circumstances of the case he has failed to discover any sufficient ground to justify him in advising Her Majesty to interfere with the due course of the law.

For the Bentley family, the last and blackest phase of the nightmare had begun. As William Bentley recalled, 'I do not want to describe what happened to my wife and daughter after I had read the letter out to them, but I shall hear their screams as long as

I live.' The vigilantes, in their fantasies of the autumn, had looked forward to quite a different scene of satisfying retribution. Screams of horror from innocent women had not been part of their longed for justice. Mrs Bentley and her daughter were attended at once by a doctor who sedated them during the rest of their ordeal.

This was necessary, if only in order that they should be able to make their final visits to their son and brother in Wandsworth prison. They went later that same day. Derek Bentley behaved with considerable dignity and courage. He assured his parents that he was not afraid to die because he knew he was innocent of murder. 'As long as you keep your chin up,' he told them, 'I'll keep mine up, whatever happens.' Only once during the visit did he appear to lose his composure, begging them, 'Help me, please help me!' It seems uncertain until this point how clearly he grasped the peril of his situation or whether he understood fully what was now going to be done to him. Iris Bentley brought from the death cell her brother's message to the public, which appeared in the *Daily Telegraph* on Tuesday morning, twenty-four hours before the time set for his execution. It sounded as if the phrases might have been suggested by his parents.

> No man's death is on my conscience. I know I did wrong in going with Chris Craig, but I killed nobody. I never intended killing anyone. Please help me.

On Monday, two days before he was due to be hanged, events and opinion moved quickly. In the House of Commons, Sidney Silverman put down a motion with the support of fifty MPs. Before the following evening, the *Daily Telegraph* reported, its sentiments had the support of two hundred members of parliament. Silverman moved that:

> This House respectfully dissents from the opinion of the Home Secretary that there were no sufficient reasons for advising the exercise of the Royal Clemency in the case of Derek Bentley; and urges him to reconsider the matter so as to give effect to the recommendation of the jury and to the

expressed view of the Lord Chief Justice that Bentley's guilt was less than that of his co-defendant Craig.

Silverman took his motion to the Table Office, according to parliamentary procedure, just after 7pm on the evening of Monday 26 January. He remained on the premises for another hour and a half, during which he received no query as to its wording or its propriety. It would be debated on the following day, the last full day before the execution. At the very least, it seemed likely that a substantial number of MPs would vote in its favour, far too many to allow Maxwell Fyfe to get away unscathed. If all two hundred sympathisers voted, it might even be difficult for the motion to be defeated by a convincing majority. It was supported by members of all parties, including ten Privy Councillors, a former Solicitor-General, and a former Under-Secretary of State at the Home Office.

From yet another direction came an attempt to help Bentley and his family. Christopher Craig was understandably in a state of emotional crisis, to the extent of insisting that he wished to die with Bentley. Through his mother, he offered 'new evidence' in a last minute attempt to save his companion. Bentley had not shouted, 'Let him have it, Chris!' It was impossible because, in any case, Bentley had always called Craig 'Kiddo' or 'Kid.' As it happened, Bentley also called him 'Chris' on occasion but anything that might halt the execution was worth trying now. Craig added that Bentley had never made the remark, 'He's got a .45 Colt and plenty of bloody ammunition too.' On the following day, Mrs Craig and Mr Bentley went together to the Home Office to offer this new evidence, which was neither new nor evidence.

The press gathered outside the house in Fairview Road, keeping their death-watch as surely as the warders in the cell at Wandsworth. Reporters, who seemed overwhelmingly sympathetic, accompanied Mr Bentley and the others on these expeditions. On the last day of his son's life, Mr Bentley went early to the Home Office. He sent a telegram to the Prime Minister, Winston Churchill, who was returning from the United States and a winter holiday on the *Queen Mary*, asking him to get the execution postponed while the new evidence was considered. Churchill had no intention of intervening. He sent a reply, telling Mr Bentley that he had forwarded the telegram to Maxwell Fyfe without comment. This particular snub re-directed Mr Bentley to the very administrative cul-de-sac from which he was trying to escape.

Unlike Churchill, the British people began to give signs that they were disturbed and even appalled by the manner in which the 'due course of law' was proceeding. It was thought prudent to double the guard on the rooms in Gray's Inn, where Maxwell Fyfe and his wife were then living. 'You have to be really brave,' said Lady Maxwell Fyfe afterwards, 'There were an awful lot of threats on his life at that time.' Rather more evident, on the day before the execution was to take place, were the gatherings of groups of people intent upon demonstrating against the taking of Derek Bentley's life.

So far as public opinion could be judged, it was running massively in favour of a reprieve. Sidney Silverman's mailbag was 200-1 in favour of sparing Bentley's life. The Home Office was receiving sackfuls of letters and hundreds of telegrams in similar proportions. MPs were getting letters and, as the day went by, phones rang and rang. The Maxwell Fyfes had to halt all incoming calls. Whatever the press stories of the autumn had suggested, it seemed that Maxwell Fyfe and his advisers had badly misjudged the temper of the nation. If the aim had been to avoid bringing the law into hatred and contempt by hanging Bentley, it could scarcely have been more misguided. The smooth Mussolini head of Maxwell Fyfe was what the new generation saw, not the merely insensitive but industrious Scottish lawyer. Contempt and antipathy towards men like Maxwell Fyfe and Goddard soon coloured the views of many young adults of the 1950s, who had no great sympathy for the type of Bentley or Craig.

When the House of Commons sat on that Tuesday afternoon, Sidney Silverman got up to ask why the motion that he had tabled was not on the order paper. The chamber was almost as packed as on Budget Day, according to the press, members gathering at the bar of the house and behind the Speaker's chair. 'Over the debate was the sharp shadow of urgency, of last minute desperation, and deep feeling.' On the Treasury Bench sat Anthony Eden, acting Prime Minister in Churchill's absence. Next to him was Maxwell Fyfe. 'Throughout the wrangling,' reported the next morning's papers, 'he sat, outwardly impassive, in formal black coat and striped trousers, arms folded across his chest.'

Silverman, a short white-haired figure, spoke from the opposition front bench. Each time that he sat down during the argument, he was passed a steady stream of telegrams. They were arriving from all over the country, urging him to get Bentley reprieved. 'The litter of telegram envelopes spread like a yellow carpet around Mr Silverman, some spilling beyond the red "swordline" over which MPs must not tread while speaking.'

The Speaker, W. S. Morrison, a former Conservative, informed Silverman that his motion was out of order and could not be debated. There followed a debate as to why the motion could not be debated. Silverman argued with passion, then paused to find a precedent in his volume of Erskine May. It eluded him for a moment and, as the press reported, there was 'the first hard hint of rancour.' A number of Conservative MPs were there to make sure that 'justice was done' and Bentley hanged. As Silverman fumbled with Erskine May they began to laugh and jeer at him, which in turn provoked shouts of anger from the Labour benches. Silverman went on to make his main point. To remove the motion from the order paper was to deny MPs a right to discuss a matter of urgent public importance. Silverman agreed that it would be improper for the legislature to seek to influence the Home Secretary while he was making his decision. But once the Home Secretary made up his mind on the matter of a reprieve, as Maxwell Fyfe had done four days earlier, then he could be challenged. He was not above parliament or the law but a minister answerable to parliament.

'I venture to think that if it were possible to put such a matter to the vote today, there would be an overwhelming majority of this House who would think that the Home Secretary had acted wrongly.' And Silverman concluded by informing the Speaker that 'you exceeded your authority in seeking to withhold this Motion from the Order Paper.'

The murmurs of agreement and dissent were stilled as the Speaker rose and gave his ruling to the crowded benches. He spoke, according to those who saw him, with 'evident emotion.'

'While a capital sentence is pending, the matter should not be discussed in the House.'

There was 'a sudden cry and a mixture of gasps and "Ohs," ' from MPs dismayed by the decision. Silverman and Reginald Paget tried again. Paget produced what was perhaps the best summary of the argument.

'I think the great condemnation which we made of the German people was that they stood aside and did nothing when dreadful things happened. We are a sovereign assembly. A three-quarter-witted boy of 19 is to be hanged for a murder he did not commit, and which was committed 15 minutes after he was arrested. Can we be made to keep silent when a thing as horrible and as shocking as this is to happen? I ask your guidance because I feel that the great mass of hon. Members here feel with me that we ought to be provided with an opportunity to try to prevent this dreadful thing from happening.'

This was too much for some representatives of law and order on the Conservative benches, who began to interrupt him. Ill-temper soon spread, and when another Labour MP, Leslie Hale, got up it was to accuse the Speaker of apparent collusion with Maxwell Fyfe. The Speaker had put himself in a position 'which makes it possible for us to suggest that he is protecting a Minister or a Government.' This time there was anger in the shouts from the Conservative benches. Maxwell Fyfe sat at the centre of the row of cabinet ministers, bleak and silent. It was clear that the case for Bentley would get nowhere in the House of Commons. Yet at the same time, Maxwell Fyfe was witnessing the destruction of his own reputation and the framing of his political obituary. Ever afterwards, he would be famous for one thing. His part in the execution of Derek Bentley.

The nightmare which had enveloped the Bentley family now

assumed qualities of Jonathan Swift and Lewis Carroll again. The Speaker had ruled that it was perfectly proper to urge the Home Secretary to remit a prison sentence. But a death sentence must not be discussed 'while the sentence is pending.' Morrison refused to 'play fast and loose' with the rules of the house. However, he made a concession which seemed to take the discussion further still into the realms of utter unreality.

'My ruling last night by no means prevents the House from taking cognizance of this matter. A motion can be put down on this subject when the sentence has been executed.'

There was an instant during which some MPs must have wondered whether they had heard him correctly. They had done. Several of them shouted out, 'Too late!'

But Morrison would not have it.

'Hon. Members may have their views upon it, and they may want to alter it, but that is the fact and that is the law I am bound to administer. A Motion at that time [after Bentley's execution] would be in order, but the Motion which the hon. Member submitted asked the Home Secretary to reconsider his decision. Therefore it was bound to be a Motion interposed before the sentence had been executed, and that, by all the authorities of the House, is out of order.'

The ruling seemed so preposterous that it did little to end the argument. Silverman had later to explain to the bewildered and frightened father that his son must die before the House of Commons could consider whether or not it was right for him to die. They might decide then that he should not have died after all. But it was not a matter to be discussed while he was still alive.

In the chamber itself, there was a good deal of passion and indignation. Silverman, having failed to persuade the Speaker, took a torn scrap of paper and wrote on it a motion for the adjournment of the house, 'To call attention to a definite matter of urgent public importance, namely the decision of the Home Secretary not to advise Her Majesty to exercise the Royal Prerogative of mercy in the case of Derek Bentley.'

The Speaker refused to accept the motion. There was a further discussion, in which Aneurin Bevan took part on Silverman's side.

But so far as Bentley was concerned, his place in parliamentary business ended with the Speaker defending himself, 'with some heat,' against charges of having colluded with Maxwell Fyfe.

'I should like to make it abundantly clear to the House that in deciding this matter last night I received no representations from any Minister or anyone else. I hope that is clearly understood.'

After so much high drama, added the *News Chronicle* reporter, 'the whole affair evaporated abruptly, leaving the House suddenly flat and spiritless as it turned to other business.' The other business was the Argentinian trade agreement. Silverman left the chamber to explain to Mr Bentley the procedural black farce that had just taken place. The sands were running fast. By this time on the following day, unless something could be done to save him, Derek Bentley's funeral would be over and he would be lying six feet deep by Wandsworth prison wall. Indeed, the grave of this puzzled nineteen-year-old had already been dug.

CHAPTER 16

The last hours began to slip by, leaving behind them nothing that would save Derek Bentley. On the other hand, Silverman was not prepared to give up. He organised a petition in the House of Commons, to be taken to the Home Secretary that evening by himself, Aneurin Bevan, Sir Lyn Ungoed-Thomas who was a former Solicitor-General, and three other MPs.

> We, the undersigned members of the Commons House of Parliament, believing the advice tendered by you to Her Majesty the Queen in the case of Derek Bentley to be grievously mistaken and out of accord with the natural justice of the case, urge that even now you will advise Her Majesty to exercise the Royal Prerogative of Mercy so that the sentence of death upon him be not executed.

Mr Bentley left Westminster to return to Norbury. It was time for the parents and Iris Bentley to make their final permitted visit to Wandsworth prison. They were informed on their arrival that this would be the last time that they would be allowed to see Derek Bentley. Before that, when Mr Bentley reached Fairview Road, a special messenger from the Home Office had already delivered a reply to the extra evidence put forward by Mr Bentley and Mrs Craig on their visit to Whitehall that morning. It was once again signed by Sir Frank Newsam on behalf of Maxwell Fyfe.

> I am directed to inform you that the Home Secretary has given the fullest consideration to your representations, but very much regrets that he has been unable to find any grounds for modifying the decision previously communicated to you.

After that, there was the ordeal of the final visit. Derek Bentley himself continued to show cheerfulness and courage. His mother gave him a letter from a friend and a rosary. She also gave him photographs of his pets, two cats and the rabbits, the three whippets. It was less like visiting a condemned murderer, in that respect, than consoling a terminally sick child. His parents assured him that men of eloquence and influence were doing all that they could to save him. When the time was up and the family was required to leave, Bentley seemed as bright as ever.

'Cheerio, dad,' he said across the wooden partition and through the glass that divided them during these visits, 'Cheerio mum, cheerio, Iris. I will see you tomorrow.'

'I will see you tomorrow.' Was it an expression of utter confidence in his supporters or an attempt to boost his family's morale? Or had Bentley still not realised fully what was going to happen to him on the following morning?

After this, there was nothing but appeal and hope. Mrs Bentley composed a telegram to the Queen. 'There is still time to save my son. Please help me.' Christopher Craig's father sent a telegram to the Duke of Edinburgh. 'I humbly crave the Queen's gracious intervention to save Bentley from hanging.' The public mood of the autumn, as represented by the press, had vanished. Instead of vengeance upon cosh-boys and thugs, an act calculated to represent such vengeance was now the source of public disquiet. Kenneth Allsop, writing in *Picture Post*, described how the decision to let Bentley hang had produced an 'emotional upset' among the British people that he had known only twice before. At the time of Dunkirk and at the death of George VI. 'At first the comparison seems irreverently incongruous. Yet the situation was very similar: each of us momentarily entangled in a perturbation common to all.'

The nation had been spoiling to get hold of one of the young thugs and do to him as he deserved. And now that it had got him, the nation did not much relish the consequences. The *Daily Herald*, on the morning of 27 January, reported that its postbag was running four-to-one in favour of reprieving Bentley.

Mr Bentley went back to the House of Commons. Silverman

and his colleagues arrived to present the parliamentary petition at the Home Office. Maxwell Fyfe had already gone home to dinner in Gray's Inn. He returned, received the petition and listened for forty-five minutes. 'Bevan argued simply, and with great subtlety and skill,' he wrote afterwards, but he thought that Bevan was trying to make political capital from an 'outburst of public opinion.' To believe that the public mood over Bentley's execution was a mere quirk of opinion was a further step in Maxwell Fyfe's general misjudgment of the situation. The effect of that miscalculation was profound and lasting. By his conduct, Maxwell Fyfe was a greater liability to the supporters of capital punishment than he could ever have imagined.

Silverman's deputation left the Home Office at about nine o' clock. Crowds had begun to gather in Whitehall, the spearhead of public dissent. There came the first chants of 'Bentley must not die!' These were not people who had much in common with Bentley, nor would they have found him appealing as an individual. They were for the most part the articulate and self-confident middle-class young, who seemed moved solely by the knowledge that a wicked and cynically unjust act was to be carried out next morning in their name.

At 9.45pm, just before the house rose, Maxwell Fyfe sent his reply to Silverman and the others. He had listened to their arguments but he was unmoved. Bentley must hang at nine o' clock next morning. Tom Driberg, the Labour MP for Malden, came out to the lobby where Mr Bentley was waiting and expressed his sympathy. The last cry of 'Who goes home?' had faded along the darkened corridors as Mr Bentley and his daughter, and Mrs Craig and her daughter walked through the deserted lobbies to the St Stephen's entrance. While it was unlocked, Mr Bentley produced for the reporters a scrap of paper with his wife's appeal to the Queen on it. 'There is still time to save my son. Please help me.'

Mr Bentley showed it to the press.

'This is my last hope,' he said.

Outside parliament, just after 10.30pm, Mr Bentley found a crowd of about three hundred people chanting, 'Bentley must not die!' Others were seen by reporters 'swarming across Parliament Square.' The crowd marched up Whitehall to the Home Office. Four uniformed constables, three policewomen, and a sergeant raced up Whitehall to block the Home Office entrance. The spokeswoman for the crowd was Anne Doran, 'a 25-year-old Roehampton girl who said she was an actress at the Gateway Theatre.' She demanded to know from the police where the Home Secretary was. The sergeant ordered the crowd to disperse, adding that the Home Secretary was not there.

The crowd remained for about forty-five minutes, while a young man went off to find out where the Home Secretary lived. He came back with an address. In a chanting procession, the crowd marched back down Whitehall to Great Peter Street. It was a block of flats in which the Home Secretary had once lived but no longer did. Maxwell Fyfe had gone home to Gray's Inn and switched off the telephone after 'a few lunatic calls.' But he found that the last evening of Bentley's life had what he called, 'humorous aspects.' One of these was that 'a hostile and rowdy crowd went to serenade and demonstrate' at the flats near the Embankment. 'The only political figure left in the building was Lord Silkin, the most mild Socialist Peer who ever supported a confiscatory measure, and we could not help, even at that dreadful moment, smiling at this example of sporadic injustice.'

One crowd marched to Downing Street, another gathered on the Embankment. They asked Mr Bentley to lead them all in a march to Buckingham Palace. It was doubtful that they could do anything to save Derek Bentley but a new generation was making it plain to those in power that it had had enough of the old and cynical ways of moral justice. Those who demonstrated in Whitehall were not apologists for crime. They were generally lawful and orderly in their own lives. But their law and order had little in common with the philosophy of the political veterans in Churchill's post-war government.

Mr Bentley refused to lead a march. 'My family and I thank you from the bottom of our hearts. We shall always be grateful to you. But nothing more can be done. My son is now in God's hands.' The Embankment crowd stood in the cold midnight air and sang, 'Abide with me.' At 2am, one march ended in Carlton Gardens where its leaders asked the police if they could present a petition to the acting Prime Minister, Anthony Eden. After some negotiation, it was agreed that one man from the crowd should be allowed to hand the petition in at Eden's house, though not to Eden himself.

Elsewhere, there was a disturbance in the Charing Cross Road. This ended with the arrest of a man for obstruction. He was carrying home-made placards which read, STOP THE KILLING OF BENTLEY! and STOP THE LEGAL KILLING OF BENTLEY! WIRE YOUR MP! Next day he was charged at Bow Street.

In the cold hours of early morning, the protesters dispersed. Mr Bentley went home to Norbury. There was no more to be done but sit and wait for the appointed hour of nine o' clock the next morning.

Little more was heard officially of Derek Bentley. But as the time of execution approached, before the prison chaplain came to see him, he wanted to send a last letter to his parents. As in the case of his police statement, someone would have to write it from his dictation. A warder of the death-watch took it down for him. Its publication told the truth about Derek Bentley plainly and pathetically. It showed courage of the traditional kind, a cheerfulness he can scarcely have felt, and a confused but moving attempt to plan a future in which he would have no part. He wrote childishly of the animals and possessions that symbolised his life, the bicycle and the dogs, the pies from the café by the pond and the television sets that his father repaired. 'I was pleased to see you on my visit,' he told his parents, though disappointed that his girl-friend Rita could not come. He also revealed that the prison authorities had not allowed him to keep the photograph of his animals because it was a newspaper cutting. The small act of bureaucratic meanness in his last hours did nothing to increase respect for the Home Secretary's minions.

Even written down for him, the letter suggested Bentley's inability to sustain a single thought for very long. To read it is to be aware of the correct but kindly prison officer in the background, suggesting to the youth the next possible topic. But the courage and sincerity of the sentiments sound like Bentley's own.

I told you Mum it would be very difficult to write this letter, I can't think of anything to say except that you have all been wonderful the way you have worked for me... I tell you what Mum, the truth of this story has got to come out one day, and as I said in the visiting box that one day a lot of people are going to get into trouble and I think you know who those people are. What do you think, Mum?

Mingled with this were brave efforts at recalling the normal and shared experiences of the family.

I hope Dad has some more televisions in I forgot to ask him how things were on the visit. Dad and I used to have some fun on that one of Leslie's, he certainly had some spare parts for it... Oh, Dad! Don't let my cycle frames get rusty they might come in handy one day...

To the chagrin of those who still retained their enthusiasm for making an example of such a delinquent, Bentley showed no regret for the style of his life. Whatever wrong he had done was insignificant by comparison with the wrong that was about to be done him in return. The letter ended in a final nostalgic indulgence.

I hope Laurie and Iris get married all right, I'd like to give them my blessing, it would be nice to have a brother-in-law like him, we could have some fun together. We could have gone round the club and drunk ourselves to a standstill on the great occasion of them being married, tell him to lob out my flower, tell him to keep my mac clean and my ties. Laurie and I used to have some fun up at the pond till four o' clock in the morning, by the café. I always caught Laurie to pay for the pies, he never caught me once. That will be all for now. I will sign this myself.

He managed, 'Lots of love, Derek.' And that was the last of

him, so far as his family or the world knew.

In the cold late dawn of winter a notice was visible outside the prison gate at Wandsworth, authorising the execution of Derek Bentley that day. The prison chaplain came to the cell to spend the last hour with him. Soon after eight o'clock, a large crowd began to gather outside the main gate of the prison. This was not uncommon in itself. When William Joyce, 'Lord Haw-Haw,' was hanged there, a crowd assembled who were described by the press as patriots who had travelled many miles to be near at hand when justice was done. The hanging of murderers like Neville Heath had been the occasion for a ghoulish enthusiasm on the part of laughing and jostling sightseers outside the gates. Children were brought as a treat to stand close by when poisoners or sex murderers or women who had killed were being put to death. But on 28 January 1953 there was a change of mood that seemed commendable. This time, the crowd was not ghoulish but angry. Indignation seemed more evident than enthusiasm.

Mrs Van der Elst, a wealthy and stalwart campaigner against capital punishment, arrived in her lemon-coloured Rolls Royce. She went up to the prison gates and demanded to see the governor. She hammered the massive iron knocker on the gate before an inspector and a police constable barred her way.

'I must see the governor!' she said.

The crowd had grown to about eight hundred. There were shouts of, 'Freedom!' and 'Let her talk!' It was then twenty minutes to nine. As the hour approached, there seemed to be a danger of a riot outside the prison. At one moment it looked as if the crowd might force open the main gates and get into the prison itself. There were too many locks and bars between them and Derek Bentley for that to have much effect. All the same, it would have called into question the system of capital punishment as an expression of popular justice. The crowd shoved and pushed towards the gates. There were shouts of 'Murder!' And then the gold and blue prison clock stood at nine. The one person to whom the crowd would listen turned and spoke to them.

'Let us be with him in his moment of need,' said Mrs Van der Elst.

Bareheaded, they stood in silence. Then they sang 'Abide with me' and 'The Lord's my Shepherd.' Inside the prison, Bentley had long since finished dictating the last letter to his parents. At nine o' clock, the hangman entered the cell, a cupboard was moved aside, and the room with the gallows was revealed only a few feet away. It was said that Bentley wept silently as he was led to the trap and that he sobbed, 'I didn't say it. I didn't tell Chris to shoot that policeman.' The hangman, Albert Pierrepoint, afterwards denied this.

Bentley was dead. The crowd was still waiting, shortly after the hour, when a prison officer opened the wicket gate and came out. He began to attach the official notice in its glass frame:

We, the undersigned, hereby declare that judgment of death was this day executed on Derek William Bentley in Her Majesty's Prison of Wandsworth, in our presence.

When the words were read, there were shouts of anger and someone yelled, 'Let's get the murderers!' The crowd surged forward again. The execution notice was seized and smashed. The police and prison officers were pelted with coins and apple cores as they struggled against the pressure of bodies. Though outnumbered, they managed to arrest two of the protesters. Later that day, John Edgar Rees, a checker of Battersea, was fined £7-10s at the South-Western Magistrates' Court for insulting behaviour, obstruction, and wilfully damaging a pane of glass worth £1, the property of the Prison Commissioners. John McEwan, a labourer, was also charged with insulting behaviour and obstruction. To the rest of the crowd, they seemed like heroes of the battle. As for the damage to the pane of glass, it was overshadowed by the far greater damage to the reputations of two of the country's leaders. David Maxwell Fyfe and Rayner Goddard. They were now to become magnets for the derision and the contempt of a new generation.

Maxwell Fyfe heard of the protests outside Wandsworth at Bentley's execution, and found such conduct 'nauseating.' Silverman tried to get the matter debated again but found that the Speaker still ruled against him. There was to be no inquest on

Derek Bentley except of the purely formal kind. It was held in Wandsworth that same morning. Death had occurred by judicial hanging and there was no other mark except for a graze on the shin. At least in this case the Home Office did not make the family or friends of the hanged man attend the prison to identify the body. Two years later, when Ruth Ellis was hanged, it was her brother who was taken to Holloway to identify her body, the face carefully painted and a scarf round the neck to disguise the effects of the noose.

Perhaps Derek Bentley unwittingly did more than anyone to secure the abolition of capital punishment in England. When the news of his death appeared in the press and the conduct of the prison gate crowd was reported, there was a reaction among many people of precisely the kind that the government had hoped to avoid. To such people it seemed that honour and justice had been represented by those who sang hymns or even smashed the execution notice, while cynicism and expediency sat in the councils of Maxwell Fyfe and the judgments of Lord Goddard.

Next day his parents received Derek Bentley's last letter. On reading its brief but courageous exhortations, they might be forgiven for feeling that their own son's moral stature now exceeded somewhat that of the Home Secretary or the Lord Chief Justice. Political expediency and the retribution of the gallows had created a hero for those who knew him at the end. Such a thing would have seemed impossible a few months before.

CHAPTER 17

In 1966, after the abolition of capital punishment for murder, permission was given by Roy Jenkins as the Home Secretary of a new government for the body of Derek Bentley to be taken from the grounds of Wandsworth prison and buried in Croydon cemetery. A similar dispensation was granted for the transfer of the remains of Sir Roger Casement, hanged in 1916 as a traitor to George V and a patriot of Irish nationalism. In both cases the gesture was seen as a tacit recognition of lingering public disquiet.

There was one respect in which Bentley's fate was the more vexatious of the two. He was hanged for being an accomplice with Craig in the murder of Sidney Miles. But what if Craig had not murdered Sidney Miles? Or what if Bentley had not shouted, 'Let him have it, Chris!' after all?

In 1971, David Yallop in his book *To Encourage the Others* put forward an explanation which involved Miles being shot accidentally by a police marksman from another part of the roof. This theory depended on Dr Haler, the pathologist, finding that Miles was shot by a .32 bullet from a police weapon of that calibre. But Dr Haler's evidence was that the wound had been made by a large calibre bullet. Moreover, the sequence of events, as described by witnesses, would make it impossible for armed police to have been on the roofs by the time that Miles was shot. Craig, according to David Yallop, had always wondered how he managed to shoot Miles through the forehead as the policeman was turning away. At the very least, however, a man's head may turn to look sideways or over his shoulder at an adversary, whichever way his body may be moving. Moreover, a man who goes through a doorway as the door opens is quite as likely to do so at an angle as he is to go straight forward. If Miles was shot and

Craig was the only person shooting at that time, then Craig shot him. The 1971 theory, taken up and favoured for a while by the BBC, is neither the most plausible nor the most remarkable gloss on the murder.

Long before this, in 1960, John Parris offered an intriguing but veiled explanation of why Bentley never said, 'Let him have it, Chris!' Parris does not give the source of his information in *Most of my Murders*. But he was Craig's counsel and it would not be unreasonable to think that Craig himself might have supplied the story. If true, then it was not Craig and Bentley alone who set out for Tamworth Road on that Sunday evening but three other friends as well. Two of them turned back and went home after the failures at the butcher's shop and the electrical supplier. At the warehouse, Craig went in first. When Mrs Ware looked out of her daughter's bedroom window opposite, the two unidentified figures she saw were not Craig and Bentley but Bentley and the other unnamed boy.

On the warehouse roof, when Bentley broke away from Fairfax, it was the unnamed boy who shouted, 'Let him have it, Chris!' Certainly, PC McDonald said in the witness-box that he could not recognise the voice as Bentley's. It was Goddard who had insisted that it must have been Bentley, since there was no one else on the roof to call Christopher Craig by his name. In this version, the unnamed boy made his escape by dropping down to the goods yard at the rear of the building and making his way home. The other two boys, who turned back before the break-in, later went to a teacher at their school to ask if they should go to the police. Their teacher told them that it would do no good. In support of this story, John Parris also quotes the *Star* for 3 November 1952, 'Police are looking for a third youth believed to be on the roof of Messrs. Barlow & Parker's premises when PC Miles was shot.'

John Parris, writing comparatively soon after the crime, presented the third accomplice as not only having been present but as still being proud of it. 'If he continues to boast about it, as he is at present doing, he may yet find himself in the dock on a capital charge.' There is no indication whether this unidentified figure in the shadows of the roof was also armed. If he was, and if he was using a weapon, he might have hit Miles. No police witnesses gave evidence of shots coming other than from Craig's direction. But by then the officers behind the shelter of the staircase brickwork were sensibly keeping their heads down. If the third youth had eventually made his escape from the rear of the warehouse roof, any shots that he fired would have come from much the same point as Craig's. Indeed, at the trial there was conflicting evidence as to whether Craig was immediately to the left or the right of the lift-shaft head. It was dark enough for confusion in the matter and for PC Harrison – with a bird's-eye view – not to see anyone on the roof for a while except Fairfax. If John Parris was correct, then there might have been an armed fugitive to both left and right of the lift-shaft.

If there was a third youth, the two who were caught certainly protected him. Whether Bentley protected him with his life is another matter. By the arguments of Goddard and Maxwell Fyfe, Bentley remained an accomplice in murder however many others might be on the roof. 'The truth of this story has got to come out one day,' he wrote to his mother in the final letter, 'one day a lot of people are going to get into trouble and I think you know who those people are.' The politicians and judges? Or other members of the 'Craig Gang,' who might have been with him on that Sunday night?

At the risk of spoiling the story, it seems unlikely that he was referring to the teenagers of Norbury or Thornton Heath. In the light of the efforts made by the Bentley parents to save their son by 'new evidence,' they would hardly have overlooked something of this sort if, as Bentley wrote, they knew who was involved. In any case, Maxwell Fyfe wanted an example made and such 'evidence' would probably not have saved Bentley.

Above all, to treat the case as a matter of who else was present or who fired the shot is to obscure the central question. In this respect, it did not matter whether Miles was shot by Craig or another youth, by accident or design, nor how many teenagers set out to rob a till on that Sunday evening. Political morality not ballistics stood at the centre of the drama. Bentley, not Craig, was the focus of national attention at last. The question was whether expediency had sent him to his death, whether an act of the most cynical injustice had been perpetrated for political ends. Many people in England, probably a large majority, sensed injustice and were disturbed by it. Before the trial, Bentley had been the captured gangster who was going to get his just desserts. After the sentence he quickly became a foolish and bewildered youth caught in a snare that he did not understand.

Even the injustice was double-edged, for there was a bitter irony in the consequence of Maxwell Fyfe's actions. The dead policeman was almost forgotten in the turmoil that attended the hanging of Derek Bentley. And for that overshadowing of Sidney Miles' courage and sacrifice, the Home Secretary was largely responsible. Had Bentley been reprieved and sent to prison for the next few years, public sympathy would have returned to the place where it properly belonged.

The lesson of Craig and Bentley went deep in the consciousness of a generation. But it was not at all the lesson that Maxwell Fyfe intended, the example of violent crime firmly dealt with. It was seen instead as a demonstration of injustice, of how 'they' would 'stitch you up' whether you were guilty or not. Six years later there appeared a film that remains one of the most distinguished documentaries of the post-war years, having a style and genius to leave its television competitors standing and staring. It was Karel Reisz's film *We are the Lambeth Boys*, a sharp but sympathetic portrayal of the working-class teenage culture of Alford House youth club in 1950s Lambeth. The discussion among one group turned to capital punishment. And that meant one case and one interpretation of it.

'What about that Craig and Bentley, then? One fellow was in the copper's arms, wasn't he? And the other fellow had the gun and he was free. And he shot him. But the other fellow that was in the copper's arms got hung. And that kid'll be out. He went in when he was sixteen.'

Maxwell Fyfe's miscalculation was far more profound than a mere displeasing of what he dismissed as a temporary 'surge' in public opinion. By the plainest judgment of common sense there had been injustice and possibly chicanery. That view of the case prevailed quickly and almost universally.

After Bentley had been put to death, the campaign of the moral vigilantes went strangely quiet. Wing-Commander Bullus's bill for the reintroduction of flogging appeared briefly in the House of Commons and was heavily defeated on 14 February 1953, by a majority of 159 to 63. The Magistrates' Association had voted in favour of restoring corporal punishment. But there were so many abstentions that the majority in favour was not a majority of members. The more strident voices of moral authoritarianism died away. A few people, no doubt, felt ashamed of their part in what had happened. Some were bold enough to say so. It was then that Lord Chorley found it hard not to feel ashamed as an Englishman when he heard Lord Goddard's outbursts.

So far as malign influence upon the two young criminals was concerned, it appeared that the easy explanation of indifferent parents and ill-disciplined family life was wide of the mark in both cases. But there was still a moral alibi in the effects of cinema, books, comics, and even television. The two stalwarts of the scapegoat flock, Sex and Violence, were paraded yet again and did sovereign service.

Those who cited such causes talked as if the British Board of Film Censors and the law of obscene libel never existed. Moral vigilance, whether in the shape of 'public concern' then or the Viewers and Listeners Association since, carefully averted its gaze from an unpalatable truth. The problem in public entertainment was not sex and violence but mindless pap, which might sometimes include sex and violence but to which moral vigilance had no objection so long as it was sanitised pap. It was precisely this diet which made violence in reality appetising to the disaffected young.

In all the indignation over what it was the young should watch and read, the emphasis has traditionally been on what should be prohibited. The tone of such moral concern, based on a traditional evangelical suspicion of the imagination, was proudly philistine. Rarely was there the least encouragement to raise the general standard of what was available. Indeed, words like 'highbrow' or 'intellectual' were to be terms of disapproval among the vigilantes. There was to be room only for the bland and undemanding fare which made up 'family entertainment.' The very young and the more easily contented middle-aged were provided for. Teenagers and young adults had better join the queue at the Odeon, the Regal, or the Streatham Astoria.

The censorship of the day was irritating at its best and fatuous at its worst. When an edition of the transcript of the Craig and Bentley trial was issued in 1954, it was impossible to print Craig's taunt, 'If you want us, fucking well come and get us,' without deleting the objectionable word. No publisher in his right mind would have issued a book filled with such language. No film containing it would have passed the censor. No play that included it would have been licensed by the Lord Chamberlain. Never, on radio or television, would such a word have been permitted. It was life, not art, in which such usage and example flourished.

It was a mere instance of how strictly books, films, and television were controlled and how implausible their 'guilt' appeared. On the other hand, a new generation grew restless at the control and the public taste that it spawned. That restlessness was manifest in the new wave of novels, plays, and films, of which John Wain's novel *Hurry on Down* in 1953 or John Osborne's *Look Back in Anger* three years later were symbolic. England's Angry Young Men were to be massively reinforced before the end of the decade by the Beat Generation of the United States, in poems like Allen Ginsberg's *Howl* or Jack Kerouac's early story *October in the Railroad Earth*.

The language of Ginsberg or Kerouac, as well as the Home Secretary's moral example, made English publishers hesitate in 1957. Long before 1957, however, the ungrateful young regarded Maxwell Fyfe's moral example as a joke. While barrack room language was a subject of prosecution, the government to which he belonged registered all young males for two years in the barrack room, exhorting them that it was good for the character, that it made a man of them, and that it matured them. That they should mature was not surprising, since they were two years older at the end of it. But the parade-ground functionaries of the state addressed them for two years in the language that the state deemed criminal if it were repeated in a novel. The moralists who fretted over crudity in cinema, literature or television looked the other way. Not surprisingly, the young saw in this a comic hypocrisy and they progressively rejected the censorship embodying it.

And yet, beside Craig and Bentley in the dock was the invisible presence of authors and graphic designers, film producers and dramatists, who had surely made these youths what they were. Did they not, afterwards, have serious charges to answer?

Enough was known of Bentley's tastes to absolve him from being an addict of cinema or crime comic violence. Even had he been so inclined, his two most impressionable years had been passed in an approved school away from such things. But Craig, after all, had pulled the trigger and it was the influence of popular culture on him that seemed the more important. On the evening that the trial ended, Croydon Education Committee received a report on Craig from the headmaster of Norbury Manor Secondary Modern School. The key passages were reported in the press next morning, alongside the conclusion of the trial.

Craig was admitted to this school in September 1947, from the primary department, and left in July 1951. During his five years here, he followed a normal B stream course for retarded pupils. At the time of his admission (that is at the age of eleven) he was capable of reading only infants' primers and for two years we had to give him individual attention with the aid of books borrowed from the primary department.

I formed the opinion that his trouble was not so much inherent inability as mental laziness, and matters were not made any easier for us by the fact that his elder sisters consistently read to him during the evenings.

He did, however, leave school with sufficient ability to be able to read simple prose with some degree of comprehension. His ability to write was even more limited, but I cannot go so far as to say that he was illiterate, as has been suggested.

In conclusion I would add that Craig was perfectly

amenable to school discipline and on no occasion did he show resentment to corporal punishment, nor did he evince anti-social tendencies.

The headmaster's report confirmed suggestions that discipline had been strict at the school and that the cane was used a good deal, contrary to Lord Goddard's assumptions about modern education. To that extent, both at home and school, Craig was quite the opposite of the neglected, indulged or spoilt child. Far more to the point, the literary influences upon him were overwhelmingly Enid Blyton or the other books read to him by his elder sisters, the infant picture-book primers, the junior school readers. It was all to very little purpose so far as his education was concerned. But this was a world away from the realms of James Hadley Chase or Hank Janson. As for the crime comics, there is no evidence whether Craig ever read any of them. Indeed, the argument by Dr Wertheim was put in reverse. Embodying one of the most basic fallacies of logical argument, he did not suggest that Craig read crime comics and therefore committed murder, but that Craig committed murder and therefore he must have read crime comics. The truth is that his known reading matter was quite different. If what he read was unsatisfactory, it was its infantile contents rather than its adult sensationalism which made it so.

Illiterate or not, however, Craig and Bentley were able to gorge themselves on cinema and television. It was the projected image rather than the printed page which was soon held to blame for their conduct. As usual, those who cited its corrupting influence were careful not to analyse the precise nature of the material available. Had they done so, their case might have seemed less plausible.

Here, for example, was the fare on offer on television and on the cinema screens of central London, during the weekend of Sidney Miles' death.

There was still only one channel of television, operated by the BBC. Its output on Saturday 1 November, in order of transmission, consisted of: *Children's Newsreel*; *County Calendar*; *Film*,

'*Looking Ahead*;' *Children's Television*; *The Week's Newsreels*; *Interlude*; *Looking at Animals*; '*Operation Diplomat*,' (Part 2); *Don't Spare the Horses*; *Weather and News* (sound only).

A schedule of this kind was thought too sensational for a Sunday. On 2 November, the transmissions consisted of: *Children's Television*; *The Passing Show*; *What's My Line?*; *Weather and News* (sound only). Scottish viewers were also able to see *Scotland in October* and *A Matter of Belief*. The music hall songs of *The Passing Show* were, of course, what Bentley was wathcing when Craig came to the door.

To most people between the ages of fourteen and forty, such an output was dreary in the extreme. Teenagers left the family sitting room for the cinema in droves, desperate to escape the suffocating propriety of such public entertainment. Ironically, on that Sunday evening, they could have settled down at home to enjoy a story of treachery, battle and murder, introducing a character of the blackest villainy. But this was on the BBC Third Programme, where the third part of Shakespeare's *Henry VI* was broadcast at 6.15 and the sadistic zeal of the future Richard III was revealed in full splendour by 8.15.

The West End cinemas that evening were filled by new releases, the films that would for the most part be going the rounds of Norbury, Streatham, and Croydon in a few more weeks. What was the fare offered to the teenage gunman? The vigilantes, after all, were convinced that the cinema was one of his profoundest inspirations. There were three 'X' certificate films showing, to which those under eighteen were not admitted. Two were French, *La Ronde* and *Golden Marie*, totally lacking in violence but having a slight erotic suggestiveness. Neither Craig nor Bentley would have been able to read their English subtitles. The other 'X' certificate film was the American spectacle of Christians persecuted in ancient Rome, *Quo Vadis*. That any of these deserved an 'X' certificate remains debatable.

At the other extreme that weekend were the 'U' certificate films, judged suitable for babes and sucklings even by the prudent censorship of the day. They were: *Because Your're Mine*, *It Started in Paradise*, *Limelight*, *Trent's Last Case*, *The Great Caruso*, *Big Jim*

McLain, and *The Big Key*. Such faults as they had were sentimentality and moral posturing rather than sex or violence.

Between these two groups came the 'A' certificate films, to which those under sixteen could only go if accompanied by an adult. Three were French, *Julie de Corneillan*, *L'Amour Madame* and *La Fille du Diable*. For commercial reasons, they were more likely to go the rounds of film clubs than suburban cinemas. The earnest middle-class rather than thousands of the proletariat were their audience. The rest of the 'A' certificate films consisted of *Citizen Kane*, *The Holly and the Ivy*, *Because of You*, *The Devil is a Woman*, *The Cage of Girls*, *The Planter's Wife*, *The Gentle Gunman*, *Horizons West*, and *The Bride Couldn't Wait*.

Sensational titles often disguised a blander content, as in the case of *The Devil is a Woman*, a story of infidelity made by Josef von Sternberg in 1935 and being of minority appeal by 1952. However, two of the releases had direct connections with violent crime. *Because of You* starred Loretta Young, rebuilding her life after being released on parole from a sentence for robbery. *The Gentle Gunman* was a moral fable of an IRA warrior renouncing violence for peace.

Like the myth of a crime wave, the scapegoats of the cinema screen were effective propaganda for moral condemnation until their pedigree was closely examined. Morality and even non-violence were the message of the movies, as approved by the British Board of Film Censors. On the other hand, the duty of violence against the nation's enemies was being loudly preached and officially sanctioned. The heady days of the Second World War had gone. But there were African savages in Kenya's Mau-Mau, the slit-eyed hordes of North Korea, the bandits in the jungle of Malaya, and as Mike Hammer put it, 'Russia and the slime that breeds there.' It was good to feel righteous and pugnacious in response to such challenges. There was not a breath of criticism at this from those who professed dismay at the make-believe violence of the screen. Indeed, the protests were from those reservists who argued and even rebelled at army depots when recalled for the Korean War.

In the end, the argument was not to be resolved. Evangelical morality was based upon a belief in conversion and the effect of precept or preaching on the individual. It lost none of this at a secular level, maintaining that by the same psychological mechanism inverted, audiences might be depraved by what they saw or read. Opposing this view were the descendants of Aristotle who thought that purgation or therapy was the basis of such experience. By living through certain acts in the cinema or a novel, the individual purged them from the level of reality and became less likely to indulge them.

There could be no compromise between such views, if only because the inconvenient truth was that each reader or viewer reacted individually. For every person who was more likely to commit rape or shoot a policeman because of what books or films offered, another would be fulfilled by the fantasy and so less likely to commit the crime. The final probabilities were, as mathematicians say, beyond computation (see Author's Note).

The great irony, as it appears by hindsight, was that the crime of Craig and Bentley belonged to an age not characterised so much by the cinema and literature of violence as by evening upon evening of morally-laundered tedium and hours of vapid images under the banner of 'wholesome family entertainment.' To that banner, adult culture had been obliged to bow.

The evangelical and predominantly philistine creed of moral vigilance had prevailed long before the case of Craig and Bentley and it had much to answer for. Such family entertainment as it approved offered little to the impatient teenager. Norman Parsley was, according to his own statement, bored and had nothing to do when he went off with Craig to rob the South Croydon greengrocer. Bentley, listless before the family television set, seemed only too glad to get out and join Parsley and Frank Fazey. Pap was the diet approved by the nation's entertainers. *Mad* magazine, soon the journal of the irreverent and anarchic young, pilloried cosy favourites like *Armchair Theatre* as *Wheelchair Theatre* and the give-away quiz show as a circus of the greedy and gormless middle-aged. In alienating the young and the intelligent, (to which groups both Craig and Parsley belonged), by driving them to look for thrills and transgression in reality, the bland diet of family viewing bore as much responsibility as the phantoms of sex and violence.

The assertion that popular entertainment was the root of all evil was but one of the phobias in 1952. A good many people were also convinced by those who flourished burgeoning evidence of currently fashionable crimes that were not actually burgeoning at all. The public read stories of Chicago in Croydon, old people cowering at night behind locked and bolted doors, women afraid to walk the streets, armed thugs roaming everywhere. For the most part they believed all this. If it was not true, surely the papers would not print it? It was not for newspaper readers to look up the figures and discover that the odds of any youth in the peak age for violence, seventeen to twenty-one, ever being involved in a single crime of violence great or small were about one in five hundred. It was not their business to establish that even if they themselves were victims of crime in 1952, the odds against which were about a hundred-to-one, the odds were a further hundred-to-one against receiving as much as a push by way of violence. Larceny and petty theft made up two-thirds of all recorded crime. Fraud and false pretences came second by a very long way. There was certainly no cause for complacency, but it was hardly universal mayhem. In the spring of 1953 the mood began to change. The nation had been on a glorious spree of self-righteousness and on coming to its senses was uneasy that the price had been paid by a young man's life.

The age was not unique in irrationality. Indeed, such indulgence was almost trivial by contrast with its splendid predecessor, the great 'Popish Plot' scare of 1679, when it took two years and the execution of between thirty and forty innocent people before it was decided that the Jesuits were not plotting to assassinate the King after all. There was a less momentous experience in English life of the late 1880s and early 1890s beginning with moral reformation by the Criminal Law Amendment Act of 1885 and culminating in the imprisonment of Oscar Wilde under its provisions ten years later. The voices of the press on Wilde's conviction had a certain anticipation of 1952, though the target was cultural decadence. There had been too much of what the *Daily Telegraph* on 26 May 1895 called 'nerveless and effeminate libertinage,' which had poisoned the moral air of England for a decade past. To Wilde himself, wrote the *Evening News*, 'we owe the spread of moral degeneration amongst young men with abilities sufficient to make them a credit to their country.' The prostitutes of London were at one with the press in fearing the corruption of 'the wholesome, manly, simple ideals of English life,' for they lifted their skirts and danced in the streets on hearing the trial verdict.

It is as if a moral laxative must clean the system of English life from time to time. No newspaper of 1952 felt more strongly about violent crime than its predecessor about the decadence of 1895. Whether child abuse will prove to be the hysteria of our time remains to be seen. It is uncharacteristic of any crime to leap by two, three, or four times its rate in a single year. It is not impossible. To some degree, figures for such crimes can be made to go up or down at will. When homosexual conduct between consenting adults in private was legalised, the figures for sexual offences dropped. By redefining child abuse to include emotional abuse, or 'inappropriate sexual activity' between parents in a child's presence, by including cases where no acquittal or conviction in court is required, where 'estimates' of numbers by the NSPCC or 'reported cases' are taken as actual cases, figures may rise more or less as required. Added to this, differing medical opinions and varying definitions offer a prospect more confusing to the public than mere crimes of gangland violence and far more frightening for the accused and the alleged victim alike.

That the topic seems the hysteria of our day is thanks to press reporting with banner headlines describing 'Kids in Torment' and promising a 'Register of Perverts.' CHILD SEX ABUSE SHOCK, for example, describes the doubling of figures in Wiltshire, and only the last line of the second column reveals, 'Many alleged offences turned out to be false alarms.' The crime occurs but on what scale? More or less than before? The ordinary citizen is as much bemused and misled as by the shrillness of the press campaign in the autumn of 1952, whose object was to convince the public against the evidence. And, as in 1952, compromise is out of fashion. Strong feeling precipitates a rush to take sides. Either many children cannot be trusted with their parents or the philosophy of the social services is a law within the law, incompatible with any fundamental guarantee of justice for the individual child or adult. Either the moral sense of the country and its families has decayed with frightening speed or the creation of the problem of child abuse is a means of self-advancement by imperialists of the social services who announce the spiralling figures in one breath and demand extra staff and money in the next. Either incest is a major reality of modern life, or the phobia is a backwash from that fashionable vein of feminist auto-biography in the United States between 1970 and 1985, in which memories of seduction by the father were a *sine qua non*. Either adults ought no longer to trust one another with children or the Popish Plot of the 1980s is up and running.

If there is an inevitable pattern in such things, an intensity of fear and outrage must gather until an example is made and a public injustice is done, whether it be to the Archbishop of Armagh, 'I cannot pardon him because I dare not,' said Charles II, or to Oscar Wilde brought down by baser men than he, or to Derek Bentley fumbling in the darkness of his last hours, 'I tell you what Mum, the truth of this story has got to come out one day.' And only in the aftermath of hysteria can the cost be counted.

On 28 January 1953, a crucial injustice of the post-war years ended the life of a mentally subnormal nineteen-year-old. But for many people it was not Bentley's case alone that discredited the system of capital punishment. In two more years the hanging of Ruth Ellis for shooting her lover in a moment of passionate anger produced another 'emotional upset,' not least because this time it was young children who went through the ordeal of their mother being put to death by due process of law. The moral watchdogs who had been so concerned over the effects of crime comics or gangster films on the young, looked the other way once more while the children of the condemned woman were exposed to real-life horror from which a mere writer of crime comics might recoil. To other children, in a school near the prison, it was better than a crime comic. They were said to be in a 'ferment' of excitement. 'Some claim to have seen the execution from their windows, others spoke with fascinated horror of the technique of hanging a female.'

The Lancet reported this on 23 July 1955 in an editorial on the death penalty. It cited the cases of Derek Bentley and Ruth Ellis, denouncing a system which 'punishes the innocent with the guilty.' The family of the condemned man or woman must endure 'a long drawn-out anguish far more horrible than all but the worst of murders.' In this case the children of the condemned woman, 'who must inevitably be deprived of the "normal home life" of which we nowadays speak so glibly have been dealt, in addition, a most shattering psychological blow.' The case of Ruth Ellis was another in which the Home Secretary had seen no grounds for a reprieve.

In other cases of the time, it became evident that Timothy Evans, posthumously pardoned, had been hanged for a murder he probably did not commit. There was doubt as to whether James Hanratty could have committed the A6 murder for which he was hanged but which another man claimed as his handiwork. The system had never been as strongly challenged before by suggestions or allegations that the innocent as well as the guilty might be put to death.

But the execution of Bentley was, if not the first, then one of the very few occasions in modern criminal history when the prison-gate crowd consisted of conscientious objectors to such an act rather than ghouls and gloaters. Whatever the outcry over falling moral standards in the post-war period, this was one respect in which they appeared to have improved out of recognition.

The roots of the Bentley case went deeper still. The years 1951–56 were a curious period of Conservative rule. They still belonged in some respects to the culture of the 1930s, a reaffirmation of traditional values after the aberration of the war years and the Labour government that followed. 'Five lost years of middle-class masochism,' as Kenneth Tynan was to call the post-war quinquennium. At one level the new government seemed not so much a symbol of political advance as an opportunity to allow Winston Churchill to do a lap of honour before retirement. The attitudes of the backward-looking and the entrenched illuminate the treatment of Bentley by Maxwell Fyfe.

There were still voices that the new generation, of whatever political persuasion, found strange and unsympathetic. At one extreme, Somerset Maugham announced that those who did not pay for their own university education but who received state scholarships were 'scum.' Closer acquaintance would scarcely have mollified him. Dennis Wheatley, addressing the Oxford Union in 1956, informed its members that there were lesser breeds than they, whom society must deal with accordingly. His audience would all have been officers and gentlemen during their National Service and would understand this. There was a moment of astonished silence before he was howled down.

The division in the culture of the 1950s went beyond the argument over making an example of Bentley to still the violence in teenage culture. Maxwell Fyfe ended his career as Home Secretary a year later and became, as Viscount Kilmuir, Lord Chancellor. Before that happened there occurred what Norman St John Stevas was to describe as a campaign reportedly 'undertaken at the wish of the Home Secretary, then Sir David Maxwell Fyfe, with the support of the Director of Public Prosecutions, Sir Theobald Mathew, as part of an effort to reform public morals.'

Whose morals? This time it was not the readers of crime comics nor the addicts of American gangster films. The Bentley case had shown that established law and order faced a more insidious foe, the young middle-class liberals. They were articulate and inconvenient. They gathered in Whitehall and chanted, 'Bentley must not die!' Their conduct outside Wandsworth prison was, to use Maxwell Fyfe's own term, 'nauseating.' Since the war they had tolerated sexual and cultural permissiveness. They slept together before marriage. 'In my day,' said one of Maxwell Fyfe's acquaintances and contemporaries in this author's hearing, 'if a man wanted that sort of thing, he went to Piccadilly.'

Crime comics were certainly to be 'cracked down' upon by the new law of 1955. Before Maxwell Fyfe left the Home Office, however, five of the most respectable publishers in London woke up one morning to find that they were being prosecuted for obscenity. Heinemann, Hutchinson, Secker and Warburg, Arthur Barker, and Werner Laurie stood in the dock for fiction they had issued without any thought that they might find themselves at the Old Bailey. The English book trade had seen nothing like it for a century or more. When the cases came on, there were three acquittals and two convictions, which left the situation in utter confusion. But as a cleaner-up and cracker-down, Maxwell Fyfe had shot his bolt. It was judged best to ease him out of the Home Office and into his largely ceremonial Lord Chancellorship. He remained there until the end of the Macmillan government in 1962.

And what good came of it at last, if any? However questionable or unjust, the fate of Derek Bentley would surely have taught a lesson to the young thugs, gunmen and cosh-boys. The deterrent effect of the case seemed bound to show itself in the months and years that followed. That, after all, had been the strongest argument against a reprieve. On 14 April 1954, shortly before his career at the Home Office came to an end, Maxwell Fyfe rose in the House of Commons to answer a question on statistics for crimes committed during 1953, the year that began with Bentley's execution. 'I am glad to say that the provisional figures for 1953 show a decrease of 40,570 or 7.9 per cent.'

There was no doubt of it. Larceny or petty theft was down by almost ten per cent. Breaking and entering was down by about the same. More serious robbery was down, though by a rather disappointing two per cent. There was a nine per cent increase in sexual offences, but that was no doubt the result of a new defiance by homosexuals or what Lord Goddard fulminated against as 'buggers' clubs,' whose members appeared before him up and down the country. (He was to regret this description, as he admitted, when the letters began to arrive asking him in confidence for the addresses of these institutions.)

However, the one thing that the case of Craig and Bentley had demonstrated was that crimes of violence would be dealt with mercilessly. And after all that, the deterrent effect was that such offences had actually increased in 1953 by just over one per cent. In the light of such a revelation, Maxwell Fyfe had rather less to be happy about than he suggested.

Such news was not well-received by his critics. The Bentley case – as opposed to the Craig and Bentley case – illustrated a rift that was more than opposition to a decision, a policy, or even a political party. Newer and younger Conservatives were among those whose consciences demurred at some of the moral postures of government in 1951-56. When the anachronistic imperial visions, the peacock vanity of Eden, the hints of deceit and collusion, brought the government to its end in the Suez venture of 1956, the new Conservative administration of Macmillan succeeded in appealing to a new generation in some of those very areas where its predecessor had failed.

The moral and social change was widespread. Against the demands for censorship and a moral reformation the libertarian movement seemed to carry both the day and the decade that followed. The authoritarians had received a significant rebuff as early as 1954 from Mr Justice Stable, summing up in the prosecution of Secker and Warburg for publishing Stanley Kauffman's novel *The Philanderer*. 'Are we going to say in England that our contemporary literature is to be measured by what is suitable for the fourteen-year-old schoolgirl to read?' That was exactly what the philosophy of 'family entertainment' appeared to be saying.

Dr Wertheim was soon overtaken by contrary evidence from Morris Ernst (Defence counsel for James Joyce's *Ulysses* in the American trial of 1933) and Alan Schwartz in *Censorship: the Search for the Obscene*. An investigation into the stimuli which set the adrenalin flowing most easily in growing boys turned up, 'carnival rides, driving fast cars, playing a music solo, seeing a column of marching soldiers ... sitting in hot sand or skiing or swimming.' Neither books nor comics were mentioned by the subjects. The unkindest cut of all was when the authors suggested that those most easily inflamed appeared to be the censors themselves, who believed that the entire world shared their own predilections. In

England too the censors were fair game. J. P. Mayer's *British Cinemas and their Audiences* was mined for examples. The favourite seemed to be that of the girl who was overwhelmed by a sado-masochistic scene in a film she had seen. She would act out in the privacy of her room the sequence in which the heroine was tied to a post to be beaten, allowing the fantasy to run beyond the celluloid version. The title of the piece of sex and violence inspiring this was *The Bohemian Girl*. Its principal stars were Laurel and Hardy. The childish mind was quite capable of devising unsavoury dreams of its own without the least assistance from the film producers or comic-book writers. To one eminent Victorian in his youth, a pious picture of the boy Nelson in a sailor suit had been a more self-revealing talisman than all the cinema of sexual deviation.

Impatience with authoritarianism by the end of the 1950s was a symptom of a general shift in public opinion. It was not a matter of moral conversion or a change in opinions long held. It was, rather, one generation fading and another taking its place. Within a few more years it seemed unthinkable that a youth in Bentley's situation would ever again be treated as he had been.

Soon after the collapse of the old Conservative government in 1956, the application of the death penalty was restricted in response to disquiet among all political parties. In 1957, the Homicide Act created two classes of murder, capital and non-capital. Sentence of death was retained for the murder of a police officer or prison officer on duty; murder by shooting or explosion; murder in the furtherance of theft; a second murder by someone already convicted of a first; murder while resisting arrest or escaping from custody. This new law was widely seen as a milestone on the road to abolition, if only because it was characterised by the most vivid inconsistencies. To shoot a lover in a moment of jealous anger was capital. To poison the same person with cold calculation over a period of days or weeks was non-capital.

A future Lord Chancellor, Gerald Gardiner, QC, led the Campaign for the Abolition of Capital Punishment. When the Labour government of 1964 was formed, he was offered the Lord

Chancellorship and was said to have accepted it only on condition that the death penalty would never be inflicted again. This undertaking was given and honoured.

In the years that followed, it was accepted that abolition was irreversible. Yet despite the lessons of the Bentley case, those of Ruth Ellis or Timothy Evans, support for the restoration of the death penalty remains strong in parts of the Conservative party and in the person of its leader. The rank and file in 1987 demands a referendum on this, as upon corporal punishment, seeking a means of by-passing parliamentary squeamishness in a populist appeal.

Practical consequences are rarely of first importance in a crusade of this kind, but they exist all the same. If hanging were reintroduced upon the system advocated, those guilty of acts of terrorism would be among the first to go to the gallows. If the supporters of the condemned terrorists were to imitate the response of the Stern gang and other Jewish para-military organisations in post-war Palestine, the sentence would be followed by the abduction of one or more British servicemen or police officers. The terrorist organisation would then announce that the execution of the convicted murderer would be accompanied by the 'execution' of the kidnapped victims. In Palestine, at least, that threat was carried out upon British soldiers.

At every attempt to execute a terrorist, the agony of the innocent would be a subject of vivid and pathetic television coverage. The pressure on the government, on its prime minister or home secretary to retreat and reprieve, would be intolerable. That a system of capital punishment for terrorist murder could survive, let alone work, in the middle of such an 'emotional upset,' as Kenneth Allsop called the hanging of Bentley, is scarcely credible. But to make a special exception by reprieving terrorist murderers while hanging others would be to confess the defeat of law and order rather than its triumph.

All this is only to say that the world has moved on from the point at which capital punishment had anything to commend it. That opinion was expressed fourteen years ago by the man who had an unrivalled first-hand experience of the deterrent effect of hanging, an effect which was Maxwell Fyfe's expressed justification for sending Bentley to the gallows.

> I do not now believe that any one of the hundreds of executions I carried out has in any way acted as a deterrent against future murder. Capital punishment, in my view, achieved nothing except revenge.

Such was the view of the retired public hangman, Albert Pierrepoint, who twenty-one years earlier had launched Derek Bentley into eternity.

AUTHOR'S NOTE

At a time when censorship is on the march, strange grounds are chosen to show that modern writing or drama is somehow debased by contrast with the culture of the past. It is almost the literary equivalent of the belief that crime rates are always soaring as never before. The *Daily Telegraph* of 12 September 1987, for example, offers the contemporary example of the television drama *Sins* 'in which a pregnant woman is tortured and a 15-year-old girl is raped by Nazi soldiers,' and the BBC play *The Happy Valley* 'seen through the eyes of a young girl who ended the story being sadistically beaten'. As a matter of fact, Juanita Carberry's story was reality and the government of 1952 sought to preserve that decaying expatriate society, the breeding ground of such conduct in Kenya, by force of arms. However, the article goes on to contrast such modern literary horrors and the self-indulgent style of contemporary fiction with 'the great happy ending' of the Odyssey. To read Homer, of course, is to see Odysseus return home in Book XXII to slaughter his enemies. Melanthius has his genitals, as well as his hands and feet, nose and ears lopped off and fed to the dogs before he dies. Like a newsreel of the SS in the Soviet Union, the disobedient servant-women are made to wash down the blood of their fallen masters and are then hanged in a row for better effect. 'Their feet kicked for a little while,' Homer says, 'but not for long.' The happiness of the ending is a little unevenly distributed, as is the journalist's knowledge of Homer. *Sins* and *The Happy Valley* combined scarcely equal a fraction of the bloodshed at Odysseus' return to Penelope. Like most arguments of its kind, this one seems strong on rhetoric and weak on detail.

SELECT BIBLIOGRAPHY

The public story of the Craig and Bentley case lies principally in the contemporary press, reports of parliamentary debates, and the transcript of the trial itself. The private story, historical setting and subsequent comment are the preserve of individual accounts, the most important of which are among the titles listed here.

Bentley, William, *My Son's Execution*, W. H. Allen, 1960.

Bresler, Fenton, *Lord Goddard*, Harrap, 1977.

Clarke, Comer, *We the Hangmen*, Consul Books, 1963.

Cobb, Belton, *Murdered on Duty*, W. H. Allen, 1961.

Du Cann, C. G. L., *Miscarriages of Justice*, Frederick Muller, 1960.

Ernst, Morris L., and Schwartz, Alan U., *Censorship: The Search for the Obscene*, Collier-Macmillan, 1964.

Furneaux, Rupert, *Famous Criminal Cases*, Vol. 1, Oldham Press, 1954.

Haining, Peter, *Mystery*, Souvenir Press, 1977.

Hyde, H. Montgomery, (ed.), *The Trial of Christopher Craig and Derek William Bentley*, William Hodge, Notable British Trials Series, 1954.

Kauffmann, Stanley, *The Philanderer*, Penguin Books, 1957. (This edition includes the summing-up by Mr Justice Stable in the prosecution of Secker and Warburg, 1954.)

Kilmuir, Viscount (David Maxwell Fyfe) *Political Adventure*, Weidenfeld and Nicolson, 1964.

Parris, John, *Most of my Murders*, Frederick Muller, 1960.

Pierrepoint, Albert, *Executioner Pierrepoint*, Harrap, 1974.

Scott, Sir Harold, *Scotland Yard*, André Deutsch, 1954.

Shore, W. Teignmouth, (ed.) *The Trial of Frederick Guy Browne and William Henry Kennedy*, William Hodge, Notable British Trials Series, 1930.

Silverman, Sidney (with Reginald Paget and Christopher Hollis), *Hanged and Innocent*, Gollancz, 1956.

Smith, Arthur, *Lord Goddard*, Weidenfeld and Nicolson, 1975.

St John Stevas, Norman, *Obscenity and the Law*, George Allen and Unwin, 1956.

Wertheim, Fredric, *The Seduction of the Innocent*, Museum Press, 1954.

Wertheim, Fredric, *The Circle of Guilt*, Dennis Dobson, 1958.

Yallop, David, *To Encourage the Others: Startling New Facts on the Craig/Bentley Case*, W. H. Allen, 1971.